SECOND EDITION

Writing with Style

Grammar in Context

HEATHER PYRCZ

A language isn't just a body of vocabulary or a set of grammatical rules. It is a flash of the human spirit, a vehicle through which the soul of a particular culture comes into the material world.

Wade Davis

Like everything metaphysical, the harmony between thought and reality is to be found in the grammar of the language.

Ludwig Wittgenstein

There's nothing to writing. All you do is sit down at a typewriter and open a vein.

Walter Wellesley "Red" Smith

OXFORD
UNIVERSITY PRESS

OXFORD
UNIVERSITY PRESS

Oxford University Press is a department of the University of Oxford.
It furthers the University's objective of excellence in research, scholarship,
and education by publishing worldwide. Oxford is a registered trade mark of
Oxford University Press in the UK and in certain other countries.

Published in Canada by
Oxford University Press
8 Sampson Mews, Suite 204,
Don Mills, Ontario M3C 0H5 Canada

www.oupcanada.com

Library and Archives Canada Cataloguing in Publication
Pyrcz, Heather, 1951–, author
Writing with style : grammar in context / Heather
Pyrcz. — Second edition.
Includes bibliographical references and index.
ISBN 978-0-19-900790-5 (pbk.)
1. English language—Grammar. 2. English language—
Rhetoric—Problems, exercises, etc. I. Title.
PE1112.P97 2014   425   C2013-907172-5

Cover image: © Lasse Kristensen/Alamy

Oxford University Press is committed to our environment.
This book is printed on Forest Stewardship Council® certified paper
and comes from responsible sources.

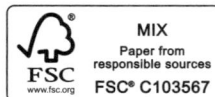

MIX
Paper from
responsible sources
FSC
www.fsc.org   FSC® C103567

Printed and bound in Canada

1 2 3 4 — 17 16 15 14

Contents

Part Four **Handbook of Style and Grammar Terms   127**

Preface to Instructors

It is a hard word—*grammar*—close to *cram* and *grimace*; *mar* is in there, and *ram*. In my experience, most students do not sit up joyously if you announce: "well, we've cleared the decks, so now we can learn some—grammar!" But for those of us who love words and the way words fit together, grammar is a joy and a wonder, and I believe we can pass on our love of language.

Over the years, I have discovered that students must acquire an under-standing of grammar before they can improve their writing. But how do you teach form to reluctant students when there is so much content to cover in any course? Professors barely have time to teach the essay format and edit submit-ted essays—and do students even read those comments? Some professors give a percentage of the essay grade to a revised draft, so students will read and apply instructor feedback. But is this enough? What do we do with students who have little grammar finesse?

Studies show that it is most effective to teach grammar in context, rather than as a set of unrelated rules and exercises. Recognizing a professor's limited time, this text is designed to teach grammar in the first 10 minutes of class—teaching grammar in context through famous quotations. The method con-sists of first breaking down the quotation into its grammatical elements, and then examining how the elements and devices create or enhance meaning, to demonstrate how the writer has used a sophisticated knowledge of language to inform, explain, describe, persuade, or entertain. Each quotation builds on the previous examples—reviewing, accumulating, and extending—to teach stu-dents to identify parts of a sentence, parts of speech, phrases and clauses, kinds of sentences and their styles, literary figures, and emphatic devices. Students are also encouraged to consider the element's or device's effect on the reader. Finally, they are asked to use the quotation as a model for their own writing—like painting the Masters.

The text is divided into four sections. The first section includes 24 lessons based on short quotations. Each lesson examines the quotation's grammatical elements with a written exercise that teaches students to use the grammatical structure from the lesson to express their own meaning. This step is essen-tial in order for the student to assimilate the information. The lesson then turns to a diversity of prompts—background on the writer, discussion questions, further quotations, and suggested readings—to stimulate a discussion of the quotation's meaning. By the end of each lesson, students will have a new understanding of how they can use elements of grammar to facilitate and enhance their meaning. These questions may be discussed in class and then further developed in a personal journal.

The second section includes nine longer excerpts. Building on the knowledge and skills students have acquired in the earlier lessons, the discussion of the longer excerpts is more complex, designed to reveal not only how the intricacies of grammar work in a larger context, but how grammatical choices determine a writer's style. Students will see that the relationship between form and content, structure and meaning, is affected by the writer's choices.

The third section, added to this new edition, is a brief guide to the writing process, specifically, writing essays. There are many handbooks on essay writing and guides to documentation on-line and in the library so I have tried to keep the section succinct, focusing on the 10 most important elements of essay writing. Many of the elements are cross-referenced with the Lessons and the Handbook of Style and Grammar Terms.

The fourth section is a Handbook of Style and Grammar Terms. This guide is integral to the book, as it provides an expanded discussion of many of the concepts introduced in the text.

Finally, for your convenience, you will find analyses of the main quotations and an index of authors and elements.

Suggestions for Evaluation
Notes to the Instructor

1. In your exam, devise one question to evaluate grammar. Give a quotation and instruct students to identify the following elements: type of sentence, mood, parts of the sentence, parts of speech, phrases, clauses, figures of speech, emphatic devices, and parallel constructions. Ask students to discuss how the form enhances meaning, and the effect on the reader.
2. Ask students to use the grammatical structures and devices they are learning in the essays you assign. For example, if you assign a five-page essay, you could ask students to use three different emphatic devices, two parallel constructions, plus a triad, all identified in footnotes.
3. Ask students to keep a journal—in response to the discussion questions, in which they also practise using the devices.

Diagnostic Test and Assessment

If possible, before reading the first lesson, ask students to write a one-page essay on a topic of their choice, or provide a topic for them to address; for example: *can terrorism be stopped?, what are the benefits—and drawbacks—of having children?, are teams necessary in university?*. Allow students a half-hour to write. Give no instructions except that they should write a one-page essay. On completion, give students a few minutes to add another paragraph about their process—what came easily, what they like about their essay, what they do not, what they would like to be able to do. Ask them to hand in both their essay and comments. Keep these assignments for future reference.

Use these essays to assess the level of writing in the class. To quickly assess each student's work, make a chart and perform a simple evaluation, using E(xcellent), G(ood), P(oor), or N(on-existent). Consider various aspects of composition: Did the student use an outline, an effective title? Does the essay have two or three well-developed paragraphs, complete sentences, and a variety of sentence styles? Are the paragraphs unified? Are emphatic or rhetorical devices or figures of speech used? Is the diction appropriate, effective?

Are there problems of tense, modification, agreement, ambiguity, abstraction, clarity, redundancy, or awkwardness? What is the level of conventional usage (punctuation, spelling)? In the language structure, where do the grammatical problems arise—in sentence construction, use of clauses and phrases, word choice, or parts of speech? Are these problems of selection or misuse? Leave a space for other comments. This assessment is useful not only for directing a particular student's progress, but also for choosing where to put your emphasis for that class. There is no need to edit or comment on these essays.

At the end of the course, repeat the exercise using the same topic, then hand back the first essays and let students compare the two writing samples. They will probably be surprised at how much their writing has improved, (some will not have improved but that also tells them something important), but they might also find that there are parts of the first essay they prefer because they were somewhat freer. Writing is an art and a craft. After one course, like playing bridge or swinging a golf club, students will likely be struggling with all the information they have received. There is a period of awkwardness as one climbs to a new plateau of skill and understanding. Like learning to skate or playing the cello, only practice will make the process come "naturally."

Preface to Students

This book is meant to help you understand the intricacies of grammar in context, in order to improve your writing skills. It is not meant as a list of grammar dos and don'ts—there are plenty of those on the market. And for every "don't" there is a writer who breaks the rule brilliantly. Does that make good writing impossible to learn? Not at all—it makes writing creative. This text demonstrates how good writers make effective choices and so, by delighting, enlighten their readers. Your essays (and the marks you receive) in all your courses will improve from your increased awareness of how words fit together.

The first section is devised to help you review the basic elements of grammar: parts of speech, parts of a sentence, phrases, clauses, kinds of sentences, literary figures and emphatic devices, but in a context that eventually throws the emphasis back on meaning. After dissecting a famous quotation to see what makes it tick grammatically, you are encouraged to examine the relationship between form and content, grammar and meaning.

As your writing skills increase, the text becomes more complex as it juggles more grammatical balls—this is the nature of writing. In the second section, longer excerpts allow you to examine a writer's style choices. You will learn how authors develop strong, distinct voices. What makes Dickens sound like Dickens? How *does* he do that?

The lessons and excerpts also provide vocabulary you need to understand feedback. Have you ever received a comment in the margin of your essay that you didn't understand? What did your instructor mean by *use a subordinate clause here or use a freight train for this sequence or this sentence loses emphasis*? How did it lose emphasis? What does one use to focus attention? What are the emphatic devices from which to choose? How do good writers do it? Once you understand what these comments mean, you will be able to use them to improve your writing.

The third section is a brief guide to essay writing. The most important thing anyone can tell you about writing an essay is to give it the time and effort it needs. You want to know how to get an A? Revise. Revision is the key to all good writing. The more effortless the writing looks, the more times the writer has revised. This section outlines 10 things you need to know about essay writing.

The fourth section is a Handbook of Style and Grammar Terms. This guide to style and grammar terminology further develops concepts introduced in the first two sections. Here, you will find definitions, more explanation, and interesting notes. Throughout the lessons, you will find words set in boldface; the boldface indicates that you will find additional information on these topics in the Handbook.

As you read through the text, remember that writing and reading are two sides of the same coin. If you want to learn something about language, something about the beauty, mystery, and joy of stringing words together, there are writers, like those introduced in this text, who can help you—writers who craft words, who string them together like morning dewdrops beaded on a leaf—simple, clear, exquisite. To improve your writing, you need to read. In this age of quick fixes there are lots of "how to" books out there, but there are no shortcuts for learning how to write. Like any craft or art form, acquiring style in writing takes desire, practice, and time. Most people fail not for want of ability, but for lack of perseverance.

Ezra Pound suggested that we write what we read. This text includes writers from a diversity of fields, men and women, national and international, contemporary and past writers selected for their ability to effectively and joyfully manipulate words. I hope they inspire you.

Notes: Where there is no source for a quotation it is attributed to the author. The following abbreviations are used to denote parts of speech throughout the text.

*adj. = adjective, adv. = adverb, art. = article, aux. v. = auxiliary verb, c. conj. = coordinating conjunction, n. = noun, pro. = pronoun, prep. = preposition, s. = subject, s. conj. = subordinating conjunction, s/v = subject/verb connection, v. = verb; verbals: part. = participle, inf. = infinitive; * = ellipsis*

Acknowledgements

I wish to thank Dianne MacPhee, Andrea Schwenke Wyile, Stephen Ahern and Greg Pyrcz of Acadia University for their generosity and excellent advice. I also wish to thank Dave Ward, Leah-Ann Lymer, J. Lynn Fraser, Andrea Kennedy, Janice Evans, and all those who worked on the book at Oxford University Press Canada for their expert guidance and many talents

I would also like to thank the following reviewers, whose helpful comments guided this second edition:

Marie-Josee Chapleau, College of the North Atlantic
Tom Gwin, Red Deer College
Wendy Morgan, Fleming College
Sheila M. Ross, Capilano University

This book is dedicated to all my former students.

Text Acknowledgements

"you fit into me" from *Power Politics* copyright © 1971, 1996 by Margaret Atwood. Reprinted by permission of House of Anansi Press.

Excerpt from Pearl S. Buck's speech, "China and the Federal Union", delivered at the Federal Union in New York, 1942.

Phil Fontaine speech delivered in 2008 to House of Commons, courtesy Phil Fontaine.

Excerpt from *The Savage Fields: An Essay in Literature and Cosmology* by Dennis Lee, copyright 1977. Reproduced with permission from House of Anansi Press, Toronto.

Excerpt from *Prisons We Choose to Live Inside* by Doris Lessing, copyright 1986 Doris Lessing and the Canadian Broadcasting Corporation. Reproduced with permission from House of Anansi Press, Toronto.

Excerpts from *Love in the Time of Cholera* by Garbiel Garcia Marquez, translation 1988 by Gabriel Garcia Marquez. Used by permission of Alfred A. Knopf, an imprint of the Knopf Doubleday Publishing Group, a division of Random House LLC. All rights reserved.

Don McKay, excerpt from "Baler Twine," in *Vis à Vis: Fieldnotes on Poetry and Wilderness.* © 2001 Don McKay. Used by permission of Gaspereau Press Limited, Printers & Publishers.

Peter Sanger, excerpt from "A Knowledge of Evening," in *White Salt Mountain: Words in Time.* © 2005 Peter Sanger. Used by permission of Gaspereau Press Limited, Printers & Publishers.

Dylan Thomas essay, "Holiday Memory", from *The Collected Stories of Dylan Thomas*, copyright © 1954 by New Directions Publishing Corp. Reprinted by Permission of New Directions Publishing Corp. and David Higham.

Literary excerpt from *Tidal Life, A Natural History of the Bay of Fundy.* Harry Thurston, Nimbus Publishing, 1990. Used by permission of Nimbus Publishing.

Part One

Lessons

The first section of the book consists of 24 lessons based on famous quotations used to help you identify parts of a sentence, parts of speech, phrases, clauses, kinds of sentences and their styles, literary figures, and emphatic devices; discuss the effect stylistic elements and devices have on the reader; and investigate the relationship between structure and meaning. You will hone your skills by writing your own examples, modelled on famous quotations—like painting the Masters. The writing exercises, which ask you to imitate these grammatical forms, will help you to increase your textual power. You will study writers' choices, discover how they use devices, and practise assimilating their form.

Prompts such as further questions, excerpts, and brief author biographies will invite you to probe the quotation's meaning. Grammar is a set of rules, inherent in the language, described but not invented by grammarians, which exists for one reason—to aid the speaker's or writer's ability to communicate. Language is a living organism, constantly in flux. It evolves. Grammar is not a bulwark, resistant to change; it is malleable, sensitive to popular usage. This evolution is what grammarians describe. Our reason for preserving a grammatical rule should never be "because that's the way it has always been," but rather "because it is the best way to express an idea." The prompts will help you to investigate the relationship between form and content—how form enhances meaning, because ultimately, it is meaning we are after.

1 Jane Austen
Parts of a Sentence: Subject, Predicate

"I have been a selfish being, all my life, in practice, though not in principle."
(Pride and Prejudice)

A complete sentence has two parts: a **subject** and a **predicate**.

The **subject** of a sentence is who or what performs the action or is being described.

The *simple subject* may be one word, a noun or a pronoun, as in Austen's quotation: *I.*

However, the *complete subject* is often more complex:

Austen's detached, ironic style has kept her current for two hundred years.

The subject can be single or compound:

- Single:

  "My sore throats are always worse than anyone's." (Jane Austen, *Persuasion*)

- Compound—two or more subjects joined by a <u>conjunction</u> but belonging to the same verb:

  In Austen's novel, *Marianne* <u>and</u> *Elinor* travel to London with high hopes.

A subject can also be

- a group of words acting as a noun:

  "One half of the world cannot understand the pleasures of the other."
  (Jane Austen, *Emma*)

- a **verbal**:

  To succeed in Austen's world requires of women courage and wits.

- a **noun clause**:

  "What she was, must be uncertain; but *who she was,* might be found out." (Jane Austen, *Emma*)

Jane Austen (1775–1817)

Jane Austen is considered one of the great English writers of the late eighteenth and early nineteenth centuries. She was born in Hampshire, the seventh child of Reverend George Austen and Cassandra Leigh. Like most girls of the period, she was educated mainly at home. Her "novels of manner," published anonymously in her lifetime, depict the middle-class landed gentry and, in particular, the provincial lives of single women looking for protection and status in marriage.

Classic Image/Alamy

Austen writes with wry humour and compassion. Her characters hope for love in marriage and, unlike Austen herself, do marry in the end. Focusing on everyday life rather than the grand events of the times, her texts are regarded as the first modern novels. It was only after her death, at the age of 41, that her brother Henry revealed her authorship. In recent years, her novels have been adapted through various media including blockbuster movies, revealing the lasting quality of her work.

- a compound clause:

  "How that visit was to be acknowledged—what would be necessary—and what might be safest, had been a point of some doubtful consideration." (Jane Austen, *Emma*)

Note the length of the complete subject of this main clause by Socrates:

The greatest way to live with honour in this world is to be what we pretend to be.

The **predicate** consists of the verb + sentence completion:

have been a selfish being, all my life, in practice, though not in principle.

Think of the sentence completion as everything else once you have identified the complete subject and main verb.

The main or finite verb is considered the *simple predicate*. It also can be single or compound:

- Single:

  Austen's detached, ironic style *has kept* her current for 200 years.

- Compound—two or more *verbs* joined by a <u>conjunction</u> but belonging to the same subject:

  Austen's characters *hope* for love in marriage <u>but</u> *accept* fate with dignity.

Hooking Your Reader

Austen's writing is not only insightful, witty, and vividly descriptive of everyday life in the 1800s, but also full of exquisite tension. She skillfully draws in her reader at the outset with her tantalizing opening sentences:

"No one who had ever seen Catherine Morland in her infancy would have supposed her born to be a heroine." (*Northanger Abbey*)

"It is a truth universally acknowledged that a single man in possession of a good fortune must be in want of a wife." (*Pride and Prejudice*)

Discussion Questions

- What is the problem with being selfish in practice but not in principle?
- A paradox is a seemingly absurd or contradictory statement, but one that can be interpreted in a way that makes good sense. Is Austen's quotation a paradox?
- How does Austen's underlying wit affect the impact of her actual words? Why is this technique useful to writers making fun of human foibles? Consider the words of literary figure and politician Benjamin Disraeli, who also used ironic wit: "There are three kinds of lies: lies, damned lies, and statistics."

Exercises

1. Write your own sentence, using Austen's quotation at the beginning of this lesson as a model. Try to replicate the grammatical pattern:

    I have been a selfish being, all my life, in practice, though not in principle.

    I have been _____ all my life, in _____ but not in _____.

    S/he is _____ nowadays, with _____ but not with _____.

2. Complete the following sentence with a predicate:

    The greatest way to live with (noun) . . . .

Suggested Readings

Pride and Prejudice
Sense and Sensibility
Emma

2 Franz Kafka
Parts of Speech

"A book should serve as the axe for the frozen sea within us." (Letter to Oskar Pollak)

To Review

✓ Identify the subject and predicate (verb + sentence completion) in Kafka's quotation.

Our next stage in understanding grammar is to identify the **parts of speech**: **nouns, pronouns, verbs, adverbs, adjectives, prepositions**, and **conjunctions**.

Begin with what you know; devise a *working definition* for each part of speech. For example:

- **Nouns** name people, places, things, and ideas (*Barack, Banff, photograph, freedom*).
- **Prepositions** show relationships: anywhere the cat can go and more (*in, through, over, among, of, for*).
- **Adjectives** modify nouns. Articles (*the, a, an*) are a type of adjective: *a/an* is the indefinite article (*a peach* = any peach); *the* is the definite article (*the peach* = a specific peach).
- **Verbs** express an action (*banished*) or a state (*is*). **Auxiliary verbs** are words that combine with verbs to indicate person, number, aspect, tense, mood, or voice: *do, be, have, will, shall*. When combined with verbs, modal auxiliaries indicate meanings such as ability, possibility, obligation, or necessity. Look at the subtlety of meaning they provide: *I could go, I ought to go, I must go, I could have gone, I might have gone, I should have gone.*

Now give a working definition for pronouns, conjunctions, and adverbs.

How would you identify the parts of the sentence and speech in Kafka's quotation at the beginning of this lesson?

subject		verb + sentence completion = predicate								
art.	n.	aux. v.	v.	?	art.	n.	?	art.	adj.	n. prep. pro.
A book should serve as the axe for the frozen sea within us.										

Franz Kafka (1883–1924)
Franz Kafka was a German-speaking writer, born in Prague of well-to-do Jewish parents. He died at 41 of tuberculosis. He published only a few stories in his lifetime; his friend Max Brod published the rest after Kafka's death, against the writer's expressed wishes. Brod's decision proposes an interesting moral question: should the friend of a writer burn the writer's works on his or her death if asked? Kafka was barely known when he died, but just 30 years later, he had been translated into 30 languages. The British writer and critic W.H. Auden claimed, "Had one to name the author who comes nearest to bearing the same kind of relation to our age as Dante, Shakespeare and Goethe bore to theirs, Kafka is the first one would think of."

Pictorial Press Ltd./Alamy

Kafka's most famous story, *The Metamorphosis*, tells of a man named Gregor, who one morning wakes up as a gigantic bug. Absurd? Yes, but the story's situation is very revealing about Kafka's theory of the human condition: we are powerless (and repulsive) as vermin, and we will ultimately be swept into the garbage. Kafka also envisioned the human consequences when we embrace the logic of mass production. He would probably have some interesting things to say about our dependence on technology.

When we say that something is "Kafkaesque," we refer to helplessness in the face of anonymous authority—from the hospital waiting room (we've all been there) to the interrogation room. A familiar Kafkian image is that of an empty, endless institutional hallway, where we don't know why we're there or where we're going. Kafka was a master at creating nightmarish *angst*.

How would you identify *as* and *for*? For can be a conjunction or a preposition—we must decide which by the role it plays. Conjunctions join words or phrases or clauses—as *or* just did. Prepositions *always* take objects because they express a relation between a noun and some other word or element, either concrete or abstract: *on the floor, in conclusion*.

Now try to identify the parts of a sentence and the parts of speech in the following quotation by Kafka:

"The history of mankind is the instant between two strides taken by a traveller."
(*The Blue Octavo Notebooks*)

For more information on verbals such as *taken*, see the Handbook of Style and Grammar Terms (127).

Try the following techniques if you are having difficulty identifying parts of speech:

- Substitute another word for the one you can't identify: for example, *instant* could be replaced with *distance*, which might be easier to identify. (The article signals a noun.)
- Use the elimination method: *between* in this example is not a noun, pronoun, verb, adverb, or adjective. Now you have your problem simplified—preposition or conjunction?
- Try to figure out the role the word plays: think of your working definitions—is it a linking word or somewhere the cat can go? Consult a dictionary.

Context

Note the following excerpt from a letter Kafka wrote to Oskar Pollak on 27 January 1904. Does this larger context alter the meaning of the quotation for you? He wrote:

Altogether, I think we ought to read only books that bite and sting us. If the book we are reading does not shake us awake like a blow to the skull, why bother reading it in the first place? So that it can make us happy, as you put it? Good God, we'd be just as happy if we had no books at all; books that make us happy we could, in a pinch, also write ourselves. What we need are books that hit us like a most painful misfortune, like the death of someone we loved more than ourselves, that make us feel as though we had been banished to the woods, far from any human presence, like a suicide. A book should serve as the axe for the frozen sea within us. That is what I believe.

Discussion Questions

- How do you interpret Kafka's quotation at the beginning of this lesson?
- Where does the textual power reside?
- What makes the quotation memorable?

Exercise

Try writing your own sentences using Kafka's quotations as models.

A (noun) should (verb) as (simile).

Examples

The future should unfold like _____.

The fear of flying will _____ like _____.

The game of soccer is _____ as _____.

Suggested Readings

The Metamorphosis
The Trial

3 Margaret Atwood
Nouns, Simple Sentences, Figures of Speech

"An eye for an eye only leads to more blindness." (Cat's Eye)

To Review
✓ Identify the subject, predicate, and parts of speech in Atwood's quotation.

A word can serve as many different parts of speech. Consider the word *hand*. We think of it as a noun, but it can also be a verb: *She handed the envelope to the courier*, or an adjective: *She is handy with jigsaws*. We determine the part of speech by the word's inflections (endings such as *-ly*), by its position in the sentence, and by the role it plays.

Nouns can be abstract (*love*) or concrete (*book*); proper (*Queen Elizabeth*) or common (*woman*); mass (*gold*) or count (*books*).

Note the nouns in Atwood's quotation:

- eye (concrete, common, count)
- blindness (concrete or abstract? common or proper? count or mass?)

There are three kinds of basic sentences: simple, compound, and complex.

As a *working definition*, a **simple sentence** contains one complete thought; one independent clause; one subject/verb connection.

Atwood's quotation is a simple sentence because it has one subject/verb connection (*eye/leads*). You can pile up subjects or verbs, but there can only be *one* subject/verb connection in a simple sentence, as in the following sentence from *Cat's Eye*:

subjects   verb

Grace and Cordelia and Carol hang around the edges of my life, enticing, jeering, growing paler and paler every day, less and less substantial.

The sentence has a compound subject, but the girls are all doing the same action (hanging around) so there is only one subject(s)/verb connection. (The other verbs are *verbals*.)

Margaret Atwood (b. 1939)

Margaret Atwood is Canada's best-known writer. She burst onto the Canadian writing stage with a startling, provocative guide to Canadian literature, *Survival*, and a remarkable book of poems, *The Journals of Susanna Moodie*, written in Moodie's voice. Since then she has gone on to write a plethora of works including poetry, novels, short stories, children's fiction, non-fiction, and literary criticism. The recipient of many honours, she was awarded the Man Booker Prize in England and twice awarded the Governor General's Literary Award in Canada.

Guillem Lopez/Alamy

Atwood often writes from a political, feminist stance, best exemplified in her poetry collections—such as *Power Politics*—and in her fiction—such as *The Handmaid's Tale*, a dystopian novel about a grim future following the failure of feminism. In *Second Words*, she states, "By 'political' I mean having to do with power: who's got it, who wants it, how it operates; in a word, who's allowed to do what to whom, who gets away with it and how."

She has been involved in cultural activism, working with the Writers' Union of Canada and PEN International to release writers around the world held as political prisoners.

If we wrote: *Cordelia hangs around the edges, entices, jeers*, then the sentence would have three finite verbs (a compound predicate), but all three verbs belong to the same subject; therefore, there is only one subject/verb(s) connection. Yet the moment we separate the subjects and verbs, we no longer have a simple sentence:

> subject/verb   subject/verb   subject/verb
> Grace entices, and Cordelia jeers, but Carol grows paler.

We have, instead, a compound sentence: in this case three independent clauses (three subject/verb connections) joined by the coordinating conjunctions *and* and *but*.

Atwood's quotation is a short simple sentence (not all simple sentences are short).

What is the shortest complete simple sentence? It must contain a subject and a verb: *She blinks.*

Why would a writer who is obsessed with words love a short simple sentence? It has three dazzling effects: emphasis (it draws attention to itself), clarity (in brevity), and variety (it provides contrast in a paragraph of longer sentences).

Figures of Speech

Simile: an explicit comparison using *like* or *as*

> "Humor can be dissected, as a frog can, but the thing dies in the process."
> (E.B. White, *A Subtreasury of American Humor*)

> "A woman is like a tea bag—you never know how strong she is until she gets in hot water." (Eleanor Roosevelt)

Metaphor: an implicit comparison, consisting of a tenor (subject) + vehicle (its expression; to what it is being compared)

What is being compared in the following quotation?

> "A riot is at bottom the language of the unheard." (Martin Luther King Jr, *Where Do We Go from Here: Chaos or Community?*)

A metaphor can also be embedded, as shown in the next example. What is being compared?

> "The need for change bulldozed a road down the centre of my mind."
> (Maya Angelou, *I Know Why the Caged Bird Sings*)

Here is Atwood's most memorable figure of speech from a poem in *Power Politics*:

> you fit into me
> like a hook into an eye
>
> a fish hook
> an open eye

The couplets (two line stanzas) are a reflection of each other. However, the meaning in the first stanza has a provocative but gentle sexual overtone, enhanced by the first trope, referring to a clasp on clothing. The second stanza shocks violently, saying something quite different about this relationship.

Discussion Questions

Atwood's quotation from *Cat's Eye* alludes to at least two other quotations: "an eye for an eye," from the Bible, and "an eye for an eye makes the whole world blind," spoken by Mahatma Gandhi. How do these allusions affect your reading? Compare the literal and metaphorical meanings of the quotation.

Exercises

1. Atwood's language can be read on many levels. In your journal, explore the levels of meaning in the *Power Politics* poem; that is, literal, symbolic, critical. What are all the ways you can interpret this poem? What does it

evoke in you? Brainstorm and then write freely. Set a clock and write for five to fifteen minutes without stopping. Do not jettison or censor any ideas. Let them flow. When you are done, take your best ideas and write a couple of well-constructed paragraphs expressing your interpretation.

2. Identify the type of nouns and the subject/verb connections in the quotations at the beginning of the lessons on Austen, Kafka, and Atwood. These are all simple sentences. Write your own simple sentence using metaphor, alliteration, and a parallel construction.

   Example: Work is a_____ and a _____.

Suggested Readings

A Handmaid's Tale
The Journals of Susanna Moodie
Negotiating with the Dead

4 James Joyce
Verbs: Principal Parts, Tense

"I will tell you what I will do and what I will not do. I will not serve that in which I no longer believe whether it call itself my home, my fatherland, or my church: and I will try to express myself in some mode of life or art as freely as I can and as wholly as I can, using for my defense the only arms I allow myself to use, silence, exile, and cunning." (A Portrait of the Artist as a Young Man)

To Review
✓ Identify the parts of speech in Joyce's quotation. Are the nouns abstract or concrete, count or mass?

Verbs are the most complex part of speech. They have many forms; however, there are *four principal parts* from which all other verb forms are constructed: the infinitive, also known as the dictionary form (*to talk*); the past (*talked*); the past participle (*talked*); and the present participle (*talking*).

In grammar, tense means time, and there are three primary, or simple, tenses: past, present, and future. However, if you want to indicate that something is completed over time, you need the *perfect* tense. *Perfect* in this context means "completed."

- Present perfect tense—completed in the present.
- Past perfect tense—completed in the past, before something happened.
- Future perfect tense—completed in the future.

To indicate that an action is ongoing, you need the *progressive* aspect.

TENSE	SIMPLE	PERFECT	PROGRESSIVE
Present	I sleep	I have slept	I am sleeping
Past	I slept	I had slept	I was sleeping
Future	I shall sleep	I shall have slept	I will be sleeping

Verbals—participles, gerunds, and infinitives—are also formed from verbs, but they do not inflect; that is, they do not change form:

- Regular verbs form the *present participle* by adding *-ing* and the *past participle* by adding *-ed* to the present tense: *walk, walking, walked*.

James Joyce (1882–1941)

James Joyce, one of Ireland's most famous writers, indeed, one of the most influential writers of the twentieth century, was born in Dublin, educated at a Jesuit school, and then attended University College Dublin. He supported his writing and later his family with a succession of jobs—journalist, teacher, tweed salesman, cinema operator, and even bank clerk. Although he also wrote poems, a play, letters, and short political pieces, he is known primarily for a collection of short stories, *Dubliners*, and his novels, in particular *A Portrait of the Artist as a Young Man*, *Ulysses*, and *Finnegan's Wake*. Misunderstood—with his work banned in his own lifetime—Joyce was and is the "writer's writer," experimental, daring, difficult, astonishing. He forged his work chiefly out of three elements: nation, religion, and language.

Pictorial Press Ltd./Alamy

Stephen Dedalus, protagonist of some of Joyce's novels, is loosely autobiographical. He embodies Joyce's search for "a meaningful pattern through the welter of circumstances" (Harry Levin). Joyce expresses this philosophy through Dedalus in *Ulysses*: "A man of genius makes no mistakes. His errors are volitional and are the portals to discovery."

Joyce left Ireland just before the Irish revolution sparked by the Easter Uprising in 1916. He wrote *Portrait* in Trieste during World War I and *Ulysses* in Paris between the wars; he was writing *Finnegan's Wake* during World War II when he died after an intestinal operation in a Zurich hospital. Given the turmoil through which he lived, it is no wonder Joyce declared, through his protagonist Stephen Dedalus, that "History . . . is a nightmare from which I am trying to awake."

- *Gerunds* are verbs in their participle form acting as nouns.

  Debating is her schtick.

- Infinitives are formed by using the base form of the verb: *to read, to write, to revise.*

  It was too late *to go* upstairs to the French class.

Identity Formation

In *Culture in the Plural*, Michel de Certeau, a French Jesuit who shared Joyce's interest in psychoanalysis and mysticism, raises interesting questions about identity formation. What activities should we choose in order to live a creative life? How do we open up the secret places of our lives, our inner desires?

How do we escape being imprisoned by social pressures? How are we to free ourselves from the cultural malaise, from the life of passivity, the silent life? How do we resist pop culture's interpretations of our lives—similar to what Northrop Frye calls "stupid realism"—mass culture's attempt to convince us of the attainability of an idealized version of our lives? He argues we are being put to sleep (think of computers, television, video games), diverted in little dark rooms, silent and silenced, preoccupied with meaningless time gobblers.

René Blouin, Canada's most ardent champion of contemporary art, once said:

> "If you behave like a mouse, you will have a mouse's life."

Discussion Questions
- What have you done in the past to establish what you are today?
- What are you doing to establish what you will be in the future?

Exercises
1. Identify the verbs and their tenses in the quotation at the beginning of this lesson.
2. Identify the verb tenses in the following excerpt from *A Portrait of the Artist as a Young Man*:

> But the trees in Stephen's Green were fragrant of rain and the rain-sodden earth gave forth its mortal odour, a faint incense rising upward through the mould from many hearts. The soul of the gallant venal city which his elders had told him of had shrunk with time to a faint mortal odour rising from the earth and he knew that in a moment when he entered the sombre college he would be conscious of a corruption other than that of Buck Egan and Burnchapel Whaley.
>
> It was too late to go upstairs to the French class. He crossed the hall and took the corridor to the left which led to the physics theatre. The corridor was dark and silent but not unwatchful. Why did he feel that it was not unwatchful? Was it because he had heard that in Buck Whaley's time there was a secret staircase there? Or was the Jesuit house extraterritorial and was he walking among aliens?

Suggested Readings
Dubliners
A Portrait of an Artist as a Young Man
Ulysses

5 Dylan Thomas
Verbs: Finite/Verbal, Intransitive/Transitive

"Lolling or larricking that unsoiled, boiling beauty of a common day, great gods with their braces over their vests sang, spat pips, puffed smoke at wasps, gulped and ogled, forgot the rent, embraced, posed for the dickey-bird, were coarse, had rainbow-coloured armpits, winked, belched, blamed the radishes, looked at Ilfracombe, played hymns on paper and comb, peeled bananas, scratched, found seaweed in their panamas, blew up paper bags and banged them, wished for nothing." (Dylan Thomas, "Holiday Memory" BBC broadcast)

To Review
- ✓ Identify the complete subject and the predicate in Thomas's quotation.
- ✓ Identify the verbs. Remember, when identifying verbs, first look for the word that describes the action or state of being: *found*, *travelled*, *understand*, *is*, *gulped*.

There are two basic forms of verbs:

- **Finite verbs** are restricted or limited by person, tense, mood, number, and voice. They inflect (change form) depending on these restrictions:

  I walk, he walks, she walked, they were walking, etc.

- **Non-finite verbs**, or **verbals**, include *infinitives*, *participles*, and *gerunds*. Verbals do not inflect like finite verbs; they remain the same despite the context:

  She yells, *running* down the hall. They yelled, *running* down the hall.

Every sentence needs a finite verb. It is an error to use a verbal in place of a finite verb.

  Incorrect: *I running* down the hall.

Distinguish the finite verbs from the verbals in the quotation at the beginning of this lesson.

Dylan Thomas (1914–1953)
Celebrated as Wales's most famous poet, Thomas also wrote the play *Under Milk Wood*, numerous scripts for films, his endearing short story "A Child's Christmas in Wales," autobiographical sketches, essays, and short stories collected in *Portrait of the Artist as a Young Dog* and BBC broadcasts collected by Ralph Maud in *On the Air with Dylan Thomas*. In his short life, Dylan crafted a wealth of poems, many written before he was 22. Dropping out of school at 16, writing full-time by 18, by 20 he published his first book of poems, to great acclaim. Living on the edge of poverty and in the graces of his patrons, Thomas dedicated his life to his art. But he led life to excess. A rigorous schedule of performing and promoting his work, combined with frequent bouts of heavy drinking, contributed to his tragic death, while on tour in New York City, of complications resulting from pneumonia and prolonged alcoholism. His writing is known and loved for its powerful energy, its driving rhythms, its dizzying accumulation of vivid details, and its remarkable craft.

Trinity Mirror/Mirrorpix/Alamy

Finite verbs are *transitive* or *intransitive*. This distinction is straightforward, once you can identify the **object** of a sentence.

A sentence consists of a subject and a predicate. One form of the predicate takes an object. In this construction there is an actor (subject), an action (verb), and a receiver of the action (object):

subject   verb   object

In repulsion, Jillian dropped the infested vase.

To identify the subject, ask "*who*": "who dropped?"

To identify the object, ask "*what*": "what was dropped?"

Most verbs may be transitive or intransitive, depending on the context. In our example, the verb is transitive because it needs an object to complete its meaning. Without the vase the meaning of the sentence is incomplete.

A *transitive* verb carries the action from subject to object. *Odin lost an eye.*

An *intransitive* verb does not require an object to complete the meaning: *Frigg wept.*

Recollection and Writing

Let's return to Thomas's essay "Holiday Memory"—a recollection of his childhood in Swansea, a way of life that, at the time of his writing, was fast disappearing. In the following quotation, there are an astonishing number of rhetorical, emphatic, and literary devices at work in this long sentence. Note Thomas's poetic use of repetition, alliteration, metaphor, rhythm, and assonance (the rhyming of vowel sounds) in his prose. Look closely at what he does with verbs—which ones are finite, which are verbals? Where does he change a verb into an adjective? What is the effect? Read the excerpt aloud many times to hear all its beauty:

I remember the smell of sea and seaweed, wet flesh, wet hair, wet bathing-dresses, the warm smell as of a rabbity field after rain, the smell of pop and splashed sunshades and toffee, the stable and straw smell of hot, tossed, tumbled, dug and trodden sand, the swill-and-gaslamp smell of Saturday night, though the sun shone strong, from the bellying beer tents, the smell of the vinegar on shelled cockles, winkle-smell, shrimp-smell, the dripping-oily back-street winter-smell of chips on newspapers, the smell of ships from the sun-dazed decks around the corner of the sand hills, the smell of the known and padded-in sea moving, full of the drowned and herrings, out and away and beyond and further still towards the antipodes that hung their koala-bears and Maoris, kangaroos and boomerangs, upside down over the backs of stars.

Discussion Questions

- Writing effective long sentences requires thoughtful ordering. You can achieve that in two ways. First by using some kind of repetition or a parallel construction (form) and second, by deciding on the best order of the ideas themselves (subject). This order will depend on the effect you want to achieve. For example, do you have a childhood haunt that is disappearing? How would you write about it in recollection—does it need Thomas's exuberance or a quieter mood? Think about all its aspects. Brainstorm and list as many concrete images that come to mind in phrases or clauses. Select the strongest and decide how you would order the concrete images to achieve the greatest effect. You might try employing another sense, such as taste or sound.
- Think about how Dylan builds tension. Once you have your ideas down, revise your use of language. What gives Dylan's sentence vitality?

Exercises

Despite its remarkable length, Thomas's quotation at the beginning of this lesson is a simple sentence. The longest sentence in literature that I am aware of is in Nigel Tomm's *The B!ah Story*, which consists of one sentence using 469,375 words—the book has 732 pages. For more information on long sentences, see the Handbook of Style and Grammar Terms (127).

1. Write a long *simple* sentence with one subject and numerous, accumulative verbs.
2. Write the longest sentence you can without losing emphasis or clarity. What grammatical structures did you use to extend your sentence? What keeps it clear and coherent?

Suggested Readings

Collected Poems of Dylan Thomas
A Dylan Thomas Treasury

6 Pearl S. Buck
Verbs: Mood

"The truth is always exciting. Speak it, then. Life is dull without it." (To My Daughters, with Love)

To Review

✓ Identify the verbs in Buck's quotation. What are their tenses? Are they finite or verbal, transitive or intransitive?

There are four **moods** that indicate how the writer thinks of his or her material—**indicative**, **interrogative**, **imperative**, and **subjunctive**. These are indicated by the form of the verb and the position of its auxiliaries:

- *Indicative*—a statement:

  "You can judge your age by the amount of pain you feel when you come in contact with a new idea." (Pearl S. Buck)

  "One is not born a genius, one becomes a genius; and the feminine situation has up to the present rendered this becoming practically impossible." (Simone de Beauvoir, *The Second Sex*)

- *Interrogative*—a question (note that the auxiliary is in front of the subject):

  "Do we participate in a politics of cynicism, or do we participate in a politics of hope?" (Barack Obama, Democratic National Convention keynote address, 2004)

  "Yet if a woman never lets herself go, how will she ever know how far she might have got? If she never takes off her high-heeled shoes, how will she ever know how far she could walk or how fast she could run?" (Germaine Greer)

- *Imperative*—a command:

  "Change your life today. Don't gamble on the future, act now, without delay." (Simone de Beauvoir)

  "Make everything as simple as possible, but not one bit simpler." (Albert Einstein)

Pearl S. Buck (1892–1973)

Pearl S. Buck is an anomalous figure in the history of American letters. Raised in China, speaking Chinese and English, her training as a novelist came first and foremost from her Chinese tutor. As she explained in her Nobel Prize acceptance lecture (1938), the Chinese novel was not considered "literature" or "art." In its early stages, rejected by scholars, it became the domain of the people and for centuries was exempt from criticism and scrutiny. It developed naturally, uninhibited, with unheralded authors. Perhaps this freedom from restriction is reflected in Buck's work.

Pictorial Press Ltd./Alamy

Buck was a prolific writer, completing more than 70 works that span many genres: the novel, the short story, autobiography, biography, poetry, drama, children's literature, and translation. She won the Pulitzer Prize for *The Good Earth* and was the first American woman to win the Nobel Prize in Literature. When she moved back to the United States, in 1934, she became involved with civil and women's rights. She and her second husband adopted six children, and in 1949 established Welcome House, the first international, interracial adoption agency. Her life was dedicated to the cultural exchange and understanding between East and West, reflected in both her writing and her actions.

Short imperative:

> "Never laugh at live dragons." (J.R.R. Tolkien, *The Hobbit*)
>
> "Dare to be yourself." (André Gide, *Les Nouvelles Nourritures*)
>
> "Unsheathe your dagger definitions." (James Joyce, *Ulysses*)

- What keeps these imperative sentences from being bossy or condescending? Note how the short, simple, imperative sentence is especially memorable. Note also that it is an exception—a sentence without a subject, rather, an implied subject—*you* (*should*). Like all emphatic devices, the imperative must be used sparingly.
- *Subjunctive*—a wish, possibility, or condition contrary to fact:

> "Virtue, in the great world, should be amenable." (Molière, *Le Misanthrope*)

Some writers think the subjunctive mood is in its death throes and we should put it out of its misery, but certain forms are still prevalent in our language—such as expressions (*God save the Queen, if it please the court, if need be*) and to emphasize urgency or importance. For a more detailed discussion of the subjunctive mood in modern usage, see the Handbook of Style and Grammar Terms (127).

Crafting Language

Buck's quotation is a good example of how to use the vernacular—informal speech, in writing. There are no academic words, no complex symbols, yet, as chatty as it sounds, the language is still crafted; for example, what happens if you leave out the second sentence? Are there words you might use instead of *exciting* and *dull*? These are content-rich places where Buck could have lost textual power had the writing become lazy. We see this careful crafting in all her writing. The following is an excerpt from her speech "China and Federal Union," delivered at the Federal Union in New York City. (The Federal Union movement proposed an alliance of the world's democracies in a federation more selective than the United Nations, an alliance that would exclude China.) Written during World War II, Buck's speech was prescient for our own time:

> [There] is a state of mind that at the bottom does not want China included because the Chinese are not Americans and not English, because the Chinese live in the East and not the West, because Chinese are yellow-skinned and not white-skinned, because in its secret places this state of mind refuses to know that the Chinese are our equals, and that, if they are in some ways inferior to us, so are we in many ways inferior to them. This state of mind is the fruit of ignorance. As an American I am more frightened of our ignorance of the Far East today than I am of any other thing. I realize that this ignorance unless it is mended will ruin us, if not in the war, then after the war, when the building of the new world, wherein the Far East will demand a place, must be done not by men foolish with ignorance but by wise men, who know the peoples with whom they must build. I find this ignorance everywhere, in the highest places in government, in places where there ought to be knowledge and there is not. I find it almost universal among the people.

Discussion Questions

- Do you agree with Buck's statement in the quotation at the beginning of this lesson? What types of truth do you think she wants to emphasize?
- How does Buck's casual style help to emphasize her deeper meaning?

Exercises

1. A change of moods in a text creates variety. Write a short paragraph discussing one of the imperative quotations listed in this lesson. Vary your sentence moods.
2. Write a number of simple sentences in the imperative mood without sounding condescending. How might you use this form in an essay?

Suggested Readings

The House of Earth Trilogy: The Good Earth
Sons
A House Divided

7 Simone de Beauvoir
Parts of a Sentence: Subject, Object

"I wish that every human life might be pure transparent freedom." (The Blood of Others)

To Review
- ✓ Identify the parts of speech in de Beauvoir's quotation.
- ✓ Identify the finite verbs. Are they transitive or intransitive?
- ✓ Identify the subject/verb connections. Is this a simple sentence?

In the above quotation, de Beauvoir uses a subjunctive mood to express her wish for autonomy, a wish to overcome objectification by others, in the human quest for individual freedom. To claim this transcendent freedom and authentic subjectivity, de Beauvoir encourages each of us to define our own identity, to choose our own creative projects, and to take on the individual responsibility that comes with freedom. First we will look at the grammatical meaning of subject/object, and then we will examine this feminist use of subject/object.

As already noted, a complete sentence consists of a subject and a predicate, and the predicate consists of a finite verb + sentence completion.

Now let's take the sentence completion and divide it into two kinds, forming two *sentence patterns*:

- Pattern A—subject, verb, complement (s/v/c): *Life is good.*
- Pattern B—subject, verb, object (s/v/o): *Freedom requires responsibility.*

The difference between the two patterns is that in pattern A the verb does not denote action—it is a linking verb. What follows the verb describes the subject or verb. In our example, life is described as good. (The verb could also be one describing the five senses—*Asian pears taste crisp.* For a discussion of verbs of the senses, see the Handbook of Style and Grammar Terms, 127)

In pattern B the verb *does* denote action: *requires*. Because it is a transitive verb, something has to be required—remember, transitive verbs take objects. The object, in this case, is *responsibility*.

Subject/Object

The subject of a sentence is the actor; whereas, the object of a sentence is acted upon (it receives the action of the transitive verb).

Simone de Beauvoir (1908–1986)

Simone de Beauvoir was a philosopher, writer, social theorist, and political activist. She contributed significant work to the fields of ethics, existential philosophy, phenomenology, feminism, fiction, and autobiography.

Her most famous work *The Second Sex* was one of the first and most influential texts of the feminist revolution and remains a seminal text in philosophy, feminism, and Women's Studies. It deconstructs women's passive acceptance of oppressive myths and roles assigned to them by society—the social constructions of femininity. Beauvoir's most famous novel, *The Mandarins* is an existential exploration of social and personal relationships at the end of the World War II. It is a fictional version of her philosophic investigation of ambiguity, freedom, and responsibility—themes she pursued throughout her life. These two books were so controversial at the time of publication that they were blacklisted in the Vatican's *Index to Prohibited Books*.

She and her life-long companion, the existential philosopher Jean Paul Sartre, form one of the world's most famous pairs of lovers.

© *Pictorial Press Ltd./Alamy*

Dismantling the Role of "Woman" as Object

Although there are many kinds of feminism, and indeed other French feminists, Simone de Beauvoir, Luce Irigaray, Helene Cixous, Monique Wittig, and Julia Kristeva are most closely identified with French feminism. Women have expressed their desires for individual freedom and equality in writing since medieval times and no doubt felt it profoundly before this. The French feminists seek to deconstruct the male construct of woman as object (the one acted upon), to revise the concept of "woman," to reclaim the female body as something positive and defining for and by women. They reject patriarchal language and seek to invent an ethical writing using their own structures and style—deeply subjective, disjunctive, impassioned, and lyrical—known as *écriture féminine*. Their style is often poetic and witty, delighting in wordplay and punning.

One of the many startling ideas that they have illuminated is how certain elements of language have subtly subjugated women for centuries. They argue that the binary oppositions deeply embedded in our language and culture—that is, in the real, imaginary, and symbolic orders—privilege the male:

Male	Female
sun	moon
light	dark
mind	body
reason	emotion
active	passive
rational	irrational
order	disorder

continued...

French feminists argue that these falsely constructed binary oppositions are a way in which the patriarchal male defines himself—distinguishing what male is by what female is not, such that "female" is understood as an absence of male presence. This dichotomy is intensified when male writers (subjects) view females as muse, the beloved, the desired (objects). Objects do not act, they are acted upon. One of the many tasks of feminism has been to deconstruct the role of "woman" as object—as the object of male desire—in order to free women as subjects of their own lives and desires. Interestingly, Cixous argues that these binary constructs are oppressive to both men and women but in different ways. Whether you consider yourself feminist or not, whether you are a man or a woman, surely this is true: one must be the subject of one's own life.

subject verb   object
Melissa flew *the plane.*

subject   verb   object
Feminist theory dismantles *patriarchy.*

The same relationship exists between the subject, the verb, and the object in more complex sentences:

In its critical analysis and subversive acts, feminist theory dismantles the hierarchies of an ancient and privileged patriarchy.

Discussion Questions
- In what ways and circumstances can one be objectified by others?
- What is required to become the subject of your own life? How is this different from becoming self-absorbed or egotistical?

Exercise
Write as long a *good* sentence as possible for each of the two sentence patterns: A (s/v/c) and B (s/v/o).

Suggested Readings
The Second Sex (Simone de Beauvoir, 2010 trans.)
This Sex Which Is Not One (Luce Irigaray)

8 Gabriel Garcia Marquez
Adjectives, Adverbs

"The interpretation of our reality through patterns not our own, serves only to make us ever more unknown, ever less free, ever more solitary." (Nobel Prize acceptance lecture)

To Review
- ✓ Identify the subject and predicate in Marquez's quotation.
- ✓ Note that Marquez separates his subject from his verb with a comma. Only when the subject is long and complex would you do this. As a general rule, *do not separate the subject from the verb*—unless there is a non-restrictive interruption, a concept discussed in lesson 19.
- ✓ Identify the adjectives and adverbs in Marquez's quotation.

As we learned in lesson 2, adjectives modify nouns and adverbs modify verbs. But our working definitions are just a beginning for our understanding of these hard-working parts of speech.

Adjectives have two specific tasks: to describe (*pale* ale) and to limit (*five* beers). They can appear in two positions: before a noun (*endless* work) or after a linking verb (work is *endless*). In this second position, the adjective is referred to as a *predicate adjective*. The words that adjectives and adverbs modify are referred to as *head words*.

Adverbs not only modify verbs (to see *clearly*), but also adjectives (a *singularly* stubborn optimist), other adverbs (he turned the corner *recklessly* fast), and entire clauses (*certainly*, we will survive). Adverbs also describe time (she danced *first*), place (they performed *outside*), manner (she spoke *informally*), degree (he played *extremely* well), and number (he bowed *twice*).

Magic Realism

As a genre, magic realism asks the reader to suspend disbelief more than usual. In "A Very Old Man with Enormous Wings," we are first introduced to the old man when he falls into a hen yard during a rain storm. But we quickly accept his wings, partly because of the objective, matter-of-fact tone Marquez uses to fuse the extraordinary with the ordinary. Marquez suggests that magic

Gabriel Garcia Marquez (b. 1928)

Marquez was born in Aracataca, Colombia, and raised by his grandparents, but because of the violence in his country, he has spent most of his adult life in exile in Paris, Spain, Mexico, and Cuba. He is one of Latin America's best-known and best-loved writers. He writes fascinating novels and short stories in a style known as magic realism—a style based in reality but infused with fantasy and myth. Marquez illustrates that "magical realism expands the categories of the real so as to encompass myth, magic and other extraordinary phenomena in Nature or experience which European realism excluded" (McGuirk and Cardwell 45). Some of his titles reflect this fusion: "A Very Old Man with Enormous Wings" or "The Handsomest Drowned Man in the World."

Peter Jordan/Alamy

Like most writers, Marquez has had day jobs—as a publicist, a publisher, a screenwriter, a public activist, and a journalist—that influenced his writing. For example, *News of a Kidnapping* is a journalistic chronicle of drug-related kidnappings in Colombia.

In 1982 he was awarded the Nobel Prize in Literature.

realism is not so much a device or genre as a way of being in the world, a cultural stance, a way of seeing. He champions our freedom of perception, and warns of the consequences of accepting, uncritically, others' interpretation of our reality.

Discussion Questions

- Where might "patterns not our own" come from? Why?
- We might rephrase Marquez's description as "the colonization by others of our perception." How does this process make us unknown, less free, more solitary?
- We think we see reality as it "really is," but perception can be false and falsified, manipulated, or reinterpreted to others' advantage. We often see not the truth, but what we want to see, or worse, what others want us to see. Is it possible to see clearly, without prejudice, uninfluenced by others? What would we need and need to know?

Exercises

1. Identify the adverbs and adjectives in the following quotation from *Love in the Time of Cholera*. Notice how often Marquez repeats grammatical structures in threes:

To him she seemed so beautiful, so seductive, so different from ordinary people, that he could not understand why no one was as disturbed as he by the clicking of her heels on the paving stones, why no one else's heart was wild with the breeze stirred by the sighs of her veils, why everyone did not go mad with the movements of her braid, the flight of her hands, the gold of her laughter. He had not missed a single one of her gestures, not one of the indications of her character, but he did not dare approach her for fear of destroying the spell.

2. Identify the adjective and adverbs in the following quotation from *Love in the Time of Cholera*, and then write your own paragraph, repeating the first three words and the exact grammatical patterns used in each of Marquez's sentences. You might choose to write on the theme of sport rather than relationships.

Together they had overcome the daily incomprehension, the instantaneous hatred, the reciprocal nastiness, and fabulous flashes of glory in the conjugal conspiracy. It was time when they both loved each other best, without hurry or excess, when both were most conscious of and grateful for their incredible victories over adversity. Life would still present them with other moral trials, of course, but that no longer mattered: they were on the other shore.

Suggested Readings

One Hundred Years of Solitude
No One Writes to the Colonel

9 André Gide
Simple Sentences, Phrases

"One does not discover new lands without consenting to lose sight of the shore for a very long time." (The Counterfeiters)

To Review
- ✓ Identify the parts of the sentence and parts of speech in Gide's quotation.
- ✓ Is this a simple, compound, or complex sentence? How do you know?
- ✓ Note that there is more than one verb in this quotation. Identify the verbals.

Simple sentences are expanded by the use of phrases. A **phrase** is a functional word group acting as a part of speech. A phrase does *not* contain a finite verb. Most often it acts as an adjective or an adverb.

Tip: To identify the part of speech that a phrase is acting as, replace the phrase with one word that will complete the sentence, then identify the function of that word. By simplifying the sentence, you will more readily see how the parts of speech fit together.

There are four basic types of phrases: **prepositional, infinitive, participial,** and **gerundive.** You can usually identify the type of phrase by its first word(s): a preposition begins a prepositional phrase, a gerund begins a gerundive phrase, and so on.

- **Prepositional phrase:**

  "We must build dikes *of courage* to hold back the flood *of fear*." (Martin Luther King Jr)

  "Envy is the ulcer *of the soul*." (Socrates)

  (Notice how the nouns are modified by the prepositional phrases in the above quotations.)
- **Infinitive phrase** (functions as the subject or sentence completion):

  "*To witness two lovers* is a spectacle for the gods." (Johann Wolfgang von Goethe)

André Gide (1869–1951)

André Gide is one of France's most influential and controversial writers. He began his career as an avant-garde writer who, after casting off his middle-class Protestant background, wrote with an unprecedented freedom about sexual matters. His work reveals a dichotomy, a tension between his earlier puritanical moralism and a freedom of sensual indulgence. Journeys played a dramatic role in shaping his life: he travelled to Algers, where he nearly died, an experience that sparked his revolt against his puritanical background; to the Congo,

Mary Evans Picture Library/Alamy

where, like Joseph Conrad, he documented the horrific abuse of the Africans by the French and Belgians, which led to reforms; and to Russia, where he was drawn to Communism—until he witnessed it in practice.

Gide was a prolific writer of tales, poetry, drama, his lifelong journal, novels (most notably, *The Counterfeiters*), travel writing, translations, and criticisms—all of which have been published in a 15-volume set of his collected works.

"The purpose of life is *to live it, to taste experience* to the utmost, *to reach out eagerly* and without fear for newer and richer experiences." (Eleanor Roosevelt)

- **Participial phrase:**

  "Nothing pains some people more than *having to think*." (Martin Luther King Jr)

- **Gerundive phrase** (remember that a gerund is a verb in its participle form acting as a noun):

  Studying French is axiomatic for students with political aspirations in Canada.

Levels of Meaning

Literature is rendered more complex than functional writing by its levels of meaning. Three levels are often identified in literature: literal, symbolic, and critical. Think of these layers as forming a well of meaning. The literal or surface meaning is the most obvious. We can take Gide on face value, that he is discussing leaving one's homeland to discover new places. However, a sophisticated reader will realize that Gide is using a metaphor to add a deeper symbolic level. Here, "new lands" and "losing sight of the shore" take on multiple meanings. Underlying these two levels is the deepest level, the critical, which, among other things, reveals the author's values. What do you think the quotation at the beginning of this lesson reveals about Gide's values?

Discussion Questions

- What do you interpret "new lands" to mean?
- On a symbolic level, what does "losing sight of the shore" mean to you? (Note how Gide's textual power resides in his use of figures of speech.)
- Have you ever "lost sight of the shore"? In what context?
- What is the significance of consenting?

Exercises

1. Phrases are important because they extend an idea, describe it, flesh out a skeletal idea. What types of phrases are present in Gide's quotation?
2. Write a simple sentence and use phrases to extend it. How many phrases can you add before the sentence becomes too heavy and collapses?
3. Revise the quotations to reflect your own opinions:

   The greatest sin is _____. Nothing pains people more than _____. The purpose of life is _____. The greatest way to live with_____is _____.

Suggested Readings

The Journals of André Gide
Travels in the Congo

10 Heraclitus
Compound Sentences, Independent Clauses, Parallel Constructions

"Everything flows; nothing remains."

To Review

✓ Identify the parts of speech, subject and predicate, kind of sentence, and mood in Heraclitus's quotation. Note that there are two subject/verb connections, each of which forms an independent clause.

An **independent clause** is similar to a simple sentence, except that it occurs within a larger structure. An independent clause has one subject/verb connection.

A **compound sentence** consists of *two or more* independent clauses. They may be joined in one of four ways:

- comma – **coordinating conjunction**:

  "One must realize that conflict is common to all, *and* justice is strife, *and* all things come to pass according to strife and necessity." (Heraclitus)

- **correlative conjunction** (e.g. *if/then*):

  "If a man begins with certainties, he shall end in doubts; but if he will be content to begin with doubts, he shall end in certainties." (Francis Bacon, *Advancement of Learning*)

  Note: The two "then" correlatives are omitted (see "ellipsis" in the Handbook of Style and Grammar Terms, 127).

- **parataxis** (a semicolon):

  "We are never deceived; we deceive ourselves." (Johann Wolfgang von Goethe)

- semicolon + **conjunctive adverb** + comma:

  "I think; *therefore*, I am."

  (This is a translation of René Descartes' *"Cogito, ergo, sum,"* from his work *Discourse on Method*, and it is not always translated with a semicolon.)

Heraclitus (c. 500 BCE)

Little is known about the life of Heraclitus, a philosopher from Ephesus, a prominent city on the Greek-inhabited coast of Asia Minor. His quotation—*everything flows; nothing remains*—has come down to us from so long ago, from surviving fragments we read through many translations and interpretations, that its meaning is veiled. Plato has the longest-standing interpretation, but it is now in question. Here is the argument, in brief, from *The Stanford Encyclopedia of Philosophy.* This text examines first a statement by Plato, then two translations of (arguably) fragments from Heraclitus's body of work, and finally a fragment from Plutarch. Plato's interpretation is based on a specific fragment; Plutarch's is not. Watch how the meaning of Heraclitus's quotation is reinterpreted and profoundly changed:

> **Plato** . . . *Heraclitus, I believe, says that all things pass and nothing stays, and comparing existing things to the flow of a river, he says you could not step twice into the same river. (from Cratylus)* . . . .
>
> **B12** . . . *On those stepping into rivers staying the same other and other waters flow. (Cleanthes from Arius Didymus from Eusebius)*
>
> **B49a** . . . *Into the same rivers we step and do not step, we are and are not. (Heraclitus Homericus)*
>
> **B91[a]** . . . *It is not possible to step twice into the same river according to Heraclitus, or to come into contact twice with a mortal being in the same state. (Plutarch)*

After a persuasive argument for the acceptance of B12 as the only certifiable fragment, we are given a new interpretation:

> *If B12 is accepted as genuine, it tends to disqualify the other two alleged fragments. The major theoretical connection in the fragment is that between "same rivers" and "other waters." B12 is, among other things, a statement of the coincidence of opposites. But it specifies*

Of course, writers like to break the rules. Look at what Soren Kierkegaard does here:

"Life can only be understood backwards; but it must be lived forwards."

Why did this philosopher choose a semicolon rather than a comma? What happens when you deliberately use a semicolon where a comma will do?

However, T.S. Eliot cautions:

"It is not wise to violate the rules, until you know how to observe them."

Kierkegaard did not use figurative language to make his quotation memorable, but he did use a very effective form called a **parallel construction**: words, *the rivers as the same. The statement is, on the surface, paradoxical, but there is no reason to take it as false or contradictory. It makes perfectly good sense: we call a body of water a river precisely because it consists of changing waters; if the waters should cease to flow it would not be a river, but a lake or a dry streambed. There is a sense, then, in which a river is a remarkable kind of existent, one that remains what it is by changing what it contains . . . . Heraclitus derives a striking insight from an everyday encounter. Further, he supplies, via the ambiguity in the first clause, another reading: on the same people stepping into rivers, other and other waters flow. With this reading it is people who remain the same in contrast to changing waters, as if the encounter with a flowing environment helped to constitute the perceiving subject as the same . . . . B49a, by contrast, contradicts the claim that one can step into the same rivers (and also asserts that claim), and B91[a], like Plato in Cratylus, denies that one can step in twice. Yet if the rivers remain the same, one surely can step in twice—not into the same waters, to be sure, but into the same rivers. Thus the other alleged fragments are incompatible with the one certifiably genuine fragment [i.e. B12].*

The passage concludes:

If this interpretation is right, the message . . . is not that all things are changing so that we cannot encounter them twice, but something much more subtle and profound. It is that some things stay the same only by changing. One kind of long-lasting material reality exists by virtue of constant turnover in its constituent matter. Here constancy and change are not opposed but inextricably connected. A human body could be understood in precisely the same way, as living and continuing by virtue of constant metabolism . . . . On this reading, Heraclitus believes in flux, but not as destructive of constancy; rather it is, paradoxically, a necessary condition of constancy (Graham).

phrases, or clauses repeated in a sentence (or a group of sentences) in an exact grammatical pattern. Parallel constructions are useful when you want to condense a lot of information or intellectually dense information into one sentence. They are efficient. As readers, we pick up the form when it is first used and then slot in the new information when it is repeated.

Parallel constructions also help make the meaning memorable. Note the efficiency and clarity in the following quotation:

"He that gives should never remember; he that receives should never forget." (the Talmud)

Discussion Questions

- What else stays the same only by changing? Do we?
- What do the various interpretations of Heraclitus's words suggest about the ambiguity of language? When might you want to leave a statement open to interpretation?

Exercise

Do you agree that everything flows; nothing remains? Using a parallel construction, write a sentence parodying (see "parody" in the Handbook of Style and Grammar Terms, 127) or agreeing (stating it in another way) or disagreeing with Heraclitus's statement.

Suggested Reading

The Presocratic Philosophers by G.S. Kirk, J.E. Raven, and M. Schofield (second edition), 181–212.

11 Oscar Wilde
Compound Sentences, Parataxis, Conjunctions

"My own business always bores me to death; I prefer other people's." (Lady Windermere's Fan)

To Review
- ✓ Identify the clauses, parts of a sentence, parts of speech, and mood in Wilde's quotation.
- ✓ Are there any literary devices at work? What makes this sentence memorable?

When writing compound sentences, choose carefully between using **parataxis** (a semicolon) and using a **coordinating conjunction** to separate the independent clauses—they have different effects. Parataxis is used when the relationship between the clauses is obvious. Coordinating conjunctions describe a specific relationship—*and* links similar words, *but* denotes a difference, or links alternatives, and so on—so you should choose precisely. Coordination can also be accomplished by using **correlative conjunctions**: *either/or, neither/nor, not only/but also, not/but.*

However, from the writer's point of view, the difference in effect is more than this. In rhythm and tone, the semicolon tends to separate, whereas the conjunction tends to join. Note with the use of the coordinating conjunction how your mind tends to hold the first clause as you move to the second clause, emphasizing the equality of the clauses, even with the conjunction but:

"One can exist without art, but one cannot live without it." (Oscar Wilde)

"Talk to a man about himself and he will listen for hours." (Benjamin Disraeli)

With parataxis there is a much stronger break. The mind leans forward after the semicolon, so that although the clauses are of equal importance, the rhetorical emphasis falls on the second clause:

"There are no dangerous thoughts; thinking itself is dangerous." (Hannah Arendt, *The Life of the Mind*)

Oscar Wilde (1854–1900)

Oscar Wilde was born in Dublin, the second son of an upper-class Anglo-Irish family. He was educated mainly at home until he left to study classics at Trinity College, where he proved himself to be an outstanding student, earning a scholarship to Oxford University. Known primarily for his nine plays, which best housed his biting wit, Wilde was one of Victorian England's avant-garde, an aesthete, socialist, anarchist, pacifist, and satirist. He was widely popular in his early career, charming England's elite with his style and wit.

Classic Image/Alamy

It was his homosexuality, in a time when it was illegal in Britain, which led to his social downfall. His flamboyant decadency became a target of moral outrage in Europe and America. Eventually he was tried and convicted of "gross indecency," and sentenced to two years in prison with hard labour. After his release in 1897, Wilde left England. He wandered Europe, unable to restore his creative life, and died of meningitis three years later.

Wilde is still regarded as one of the world's wittiest men. His works have been translated into numerous languages and adapted and performed on stage and screen.

When the clauses are very short, you may use a comma instead of a semicolon.

"The fool wonders, the wise man asks." (Benjamin Disraeli, *Count Alarcos*)

In the following quotation, the parallel construction together with the parataxis causes a rhythm that emphasizes the break:

"Youth is a blunder; manhood a struggle; old age a regret." (Benjamin Disraeli, *Coningsby*)

Subtleties in Writing

In the following quotation from *De Profundis*, Wilde arouses our sympathy not by venting anger or realistically describing his situation, but rather by expressing lyrically—through the personification of nature—the loneliness caused by societal rejection. This sense of loneliness is enhanced by his bleak thought that society not only has no place for him, but *has none to offer*. Notice how Wilde's use of a semicolon after "to offer" makes us dwell there briefly as a comma would not:

Society, as we have constituted it, will have no place for me, has none to offer; but Nature, whose sweet rains fall on unjust and just alike, will have clefts in the rocks where I may hide, and secret valleys in whose silence I may weep undisturbed. She will hang the night with stars so that I may walk abroad in the darkness without stumbling, and send the wind over my footprints so that none may track me to my hurt: she will cleanse me in great waters, and with bitter herbs make me whole.

Read the first line out loud a few times. Note how Wilde uses a compound structure to set up the distinction between "Society" and "Nature." If you were to change "will have" to "has" in the first line, the sentence would lose the emphasis on the shorter, more dramatic "has none to offer." Note also how the emphasis throughout falls exactly where Wilde wants it, on content-rich words such as *Nature*, *clefts*, and *bitter herbs*. Diction matters. Wilde wanted certain words to resound, and he accomplished this effect by crafting the rhythm. However, the whole of the passage moves toward the conclusion, "make me whole." The full colon announces that the conclusion follows. Arrangement of words also matters. Wilde would have lost his desired emphasis if he had written "and make me whole with bitter herbs."

Discussion Questions
- Homosexuality is much more understood and accepted today than it was in Wilde's time. However, many people, for many reasons, still feel like "outsiders." Can you think of situations in our present society where individuals might feel excluded?
- How honest are our contemporary inclusions?

Exercises
1. Take the following quotations by Wilde and turn them into compound sentences. Did you use a coordinating conjunction, a conjunctive adverb, or parataxis? Why?

   "The well-bred contradict other people. The wise contradict themselves." (*Phrases and Philosophies for the Use of the Young*)

   "The public is wonderfully tolerant. It forgives everything except genius." (*The True Function and Value of Criticism*)

   "Men always want to be a woman's first love. Women have a more subtle instinct: what they like is to be a man's last romance."

2. Write several compound sentences using the examples from the lesson as models. Write each sentence first using a coordinating conjunction and then using parataxis. For each pair of sentences, decide which style conveys your idea most effectively.

Suggested Readings
The Importance of Being Earnest
The Picture of Dorian Gray

12 Virginia Woolf
Compound Sentences, Freight Trains, Triads

"Is it good, is it bad, is it right or wrong?" (To the Lighthouse)

To Review

✓   Identify the parts of speech, the s/v connections, and the clauses.

A **freight train** is a style of compound sentence that consists of three or more independent clauses, often but not necessarily in a similar grammatical pattern. It has several virtues:

- It is useful in joining a series of events, ideas, impressions, feelings, or perceptions without judging their relative value, a style used frequently in the Bible to great effect:

  "And the rain descended and the floods came, and the winds blew, and beat upon the house; and it fell; and great was the fall of it." (Matthew 7:27)

- It suggests the flow of pure experience, as in the following quotation from Woolf's *To the Lighthouse*:

  "And he had never run a penny into debt; he had never cost his father a penny since he was fifteen; he had helped them at home out of his savings; he was educating his sister."

- It is especially useful when you want to get inside a character's mind. Virginia Woolf perfected this use in her "stream of consciousness" style, in which independent clauses are joined by parataxis, and extended by participle phrases and the odd dependent clause. In the following extract from *Mrs. Dalloway*, Peter ("he" in the quotation) has just come back into Clarissa's ("her") life:

  Here she is mending her dress; mending her dress as usual, he thought; here she's been sitting all the time I've been in India; mending her dress; playing about; going to parties; running to the House and back and all that, he thought; growing more and more irritated, more and more

Virginia Woolf (1882–1941)

Virginia Woolf was a prolific writer of diaries, letters, critical reviews, essays, short stories, and novels. Woolf never attended university; rather, she educated herself, reading through her father's large library and studying languages. She was a founder of the modernist movement and a central figure in the Bloomsbury Group, one of London's most famous literary circles. In 1912, she married political journalist Leonard Woolf, and with him founded Hogarth Press.

Pictorial Press Ltd./Alamy

Pioneering her own style, she wrote innovative, impressionistic novels, often eschewing plot and structure, focusing on the inner life of the character, employing a technique called stream of consciousness. In her work, she examines class hierarchy, gender issues, and, from a pacifist perspective, the consequences of war. Her essay "A Room of One's Own" is considered a major treatise on the historical, economic, and social underpinnings of women's writing.

The tragedy of Woolf's life was due to a bipolar disorder that began to manifest itself at 13, when her mother died and she suffered her first major breakdown. Usually vivacious and witty, writing intensely, Woolf would suddenly be hit with incapacitating migraines and extreme periods of depression when she could not work. In 1941, when she feared the permanency of mental breakdown, she filled her pockets with rocks and drowned herself in the River Ouse, near her home in Sussex.

agitated, for there's nothing in the world so bad for some women as marriage, he thought; and politics; and having a Conservative husband, like the admirable Richard.

- Which clause is dependent? (Hint: find the ellipsis of *that*.)

A freight train that uses three independent clauses in a repeated grammatical pattern is referred to as a **triad**. To separate very short clauses, use a comma—a semicolon is simply too overbearing—as is used in the following famous triad, attributed to Julius Caesar:

"I came, I saw, I conquered." (*"Veni, vidi, vici."*)

Notice that the word *and* does not appear before the third clause (referred to as **asyndeton**). This style choice is common in triads.

"Great minds discuss ideas; average minds discuss events; small minds discuss people." (anonymous proverb)

Polysyndeton, on the other hand, places a conjunction (*and*, *or*) between every member of a list.

> I feasted on melon and pepino and figs and mango and blood oranges right off the tree.

Discussion Questions

Persuasion is essential not only in overtly political writing, but in many forms of argument. Woolf's use of the triad in the quotation at the beginning of this lesson makes her statement memorable, but her use of the interrogative mood makes it persuasive. She is trying to convince her readers to ask questions, to think for themselves. Woolf believed that a writer's task is to see as truthfully as possible, to avoid being unduly influenced by the opinions of others or by methods of opacity used by those who, for their own ends, want to blind us. Working against the norm, her pacifist, feminist views, as expressed in the following passage from Woolf's *Three Guineas*, often caused controversy:

> Therefore if you insist upon fighting to protect me, or "our" country, let it be understood, soberly and rationally between us, that you are fighting to gratify a sex instinct which I cannot share; to procure benefits which I have not shared and probably will not share; but not to gratify my instincts, or to protect either myself or my country. "For," the outsider will say, "in fact, as a woman, I have no country. As a woman I want no country. As a woman my country is the whole world."

More than 70 years later, we are all forced to regard the whole world as our "country"; that is, our responsibility. Factors such as climate change, pollution, terrorism, overpopulation, and global economics have changed the way we look at the world. Recent wars such as those in Afghanistan and Iraq raise questions we need to ask: Who is fighting these wars? For whom are they being fought? And for what reasons? We return to Woolf's question: "Is it good, is it bad, is it right or wrong?"

Exercises

1. In the quotation from *Mrs. Dalloway*, Woolf has replaced some commas with semicolons. Is this necessary? What is the effect of Woolf's choice?
2. Use a freight train to describe your home or a concept from your discipline.
3. Write a short, tight triad in Caesar's style.

Suggested Readings

A Room of One's Own
To the Lighthouse
The Common Reader

13 Graham Greene
Complex Sentences, Dependent Clauses

"When we are not sure, we are alive."

To Review

✓ Identify the parts of speech, clauses, and subject/verb connections in Greene's quotation.

The compound sentence patterns we have been looking at (including triads and freight trains) are called serial structures, in which the clauses are treated as equally significant. However, in complex or hierarchic structures, one idea becomes paramount, and the others are subordinate to it. Inequality replaces equality.

A **complex sentence** contains one independent clause and (at least) one dependent clause. We have discussed the independent clause (see lesson 10); what then is a **dependent clause**?

When a clause is subordinate to the main idea in a sentence, we refer to it as a dependent clause. One way of recognizing a dependent clause is by its inability to stand on its own. For example, the clause *when we are not sure* has one subject/finite verb connection (*we/are*) but is not a complete thought; it is a subordinate thought, dependent on the main clause (*we are alive*) to complete it. *When* is the subordinating conjunction.

There are three basic positions in a complex sentence where you can put the independent or main clause:

- *Beginning* (known as a loose sentence): main clause + subordinate clause(s)

    "There is always one moment in childhood when the door opens and lets the future in." (Graham Greene, *The Power and the Glory*)

    The advantage of this position is clarity.

- *Middle* (known as a centred sentence): subordinate clause(s) + main clause + other subordinate clauses

    Before the water rose any higher, *I resolved to visit Venice*, if I possibly could.

Graham Greene (1904–1991)

Born in Hertfordshire and educated at Oxford University, Greene was one of the most widely read novelists of the twentieth century. In his early life, in addition to writing creative pieces, he worked as a freelance journalist, editor, and reviewer. He later became a member of Britain's spy organization MI6, which supplied him with rich material for novels such as *The Ministry of Fear*, *The Heart of the Matter*, and *The Third Man*.

Pictorial Press Ltd./Alamy

Although Greene also wrote plays and short stories, he is recognized foremost as a novelist. From the 1930s to the 1980s, he wrote popular thrillers about the political, social, and economic issues of his time. He cleverly adapted both the nineteenth-century romance thriller and the classic detective novel, creating a new, modern style to embody his vision. His novels are characterized by opening in the middle of things (*in medias res*), vivid but circumspect descriptions, effective use of allusion and irony, and a fast pace. Henry Donaghy includes in Greene's themes "the divided self," "the betrayal of a friend," and "the real presence of supernatural evil in the world" (9).

Greene was one of those rare writers who combine literary acclaim and political savvy with immense popularity. Greene has been nominated for the Nobel Prize in Literature several times, and many of his books have been made into movies.

> "Whenever people agree with me, *I always feel* I must be wrong."
> (Oscar Wilde, *Lady Windermere's Fan*)

Note that clauses are separated by commas except when they are restrictive. "I must be wrong" is a restrictive clause modifying the verb (*feel*) of the main clause. Its conjunction (*that*) is omitted (an ellipsis).

- *End* (known as a periodic sentence): subordinate clause(s) + main clause

> "When the gods wish to punish us, *they answer our prayers*." (Oscar Wilde, *An Ideal Husband*)

Notice that the end is the most emphatic position, the beginning a little less, the middle least of all. In a periodic sentence, the tension builds as the main point is delayed. For example, in the following sentence, note the effect of the rising tension as our instinct to predict takes hold:

> As we started to arrange the pieces on the board (*yes, yes*), I was startled (*by what?*) by the sight of (*what sight?*) his crippled (*what part of the body?*) right hand.

Note that it is not until the last word that the tension is released.

Tension

Novelists often use tension to drive their readers forward in the plot, and you can use this technique in your essays to enhance your argument. There are many forms of tension. As discussed earlier in this lesson, the periodic sentence creates tension by delaying the main idea. In lesson 1 we examined another technique—hooking your reader with tantalizing or mysterious details in the opening sentence or paragraph. Greene states that his novel, *The Third Man*, was developed from a single sentence, full of the unexplained, full of tension:

> I had paid my last farewell to Harry a week ago, when his coffin was lowered into the frozen February ground, so that it was with incredulity that I saw him pass by, without a sign of recognition, among the host of strangers in the Strand.

You can also create tension through meaning alone—for example, by presenting an unexpected idea. The element of surprise creates tension by forcing the reader to suspend his or her disbelief long enough to hear the explanation. This effect is similar to the tension an argument generates. For example, when you write an essay, you present a unique idea—your thesis—and ask the reader to accept your idea and follow along as you provide evidence supporting your claim.

Discussion Questions

- What does Greene mean by "alive" in the quotation at the beginning of this lesson?
- What is the effect of uncertainty on you? Do you find Greene's idea reassuring or unsettling or ridiculous?

Exercises

1. Play with the two content-rich positions in the quotation at the beginning of this lesson—the words *sure* and *alive*—to see what ideas you can come up with that are unexpected, but ring true.
2. Write three complex sentences: one loose, one centred, and one periodic.

Suggested Readings

The Power and the Glory
The Heart of the Matter
Our Man in Havana

14 Hannah Arendt
Complex Sentences, Dependent Clauses, Subordinating Conjunctions

"The sad truth is that most evil is done by people who never make up their minds to be either good or evil." (The Life of the Mind)

To Review
✓ Identify the nouns, finite verbs, and verbals in Arendt's quotation.

To identify the clauses in Arendt's quotation, examine the syntax closely: the first subject, *the sad truth*, is followed by the finite verb, the linking verb, *is*. Linking verbs are a special kind of intransitive verb. Remember, intransitive verbs do not take an object. Linking verbs *appear* to have an object, but the action is not transferred; rather, the subject or verb is modified: *the car is totalled*; *the day was cold*; *the program seems complex*. The sentence completion (*that most evil is done by people who never make up their minds to be either good or evil*) is composed of two clauses: a *that* clause (*that most evil is done by people*), which modifies the subject (*truth*), and a restrictive *who* clause (*who never make up their minds*), which modifies *people*, and ends with an infinitive phrase (*to be either good or evil*).

Subordinating conjunctions are used to connect dependent clauses to independent (or main) clauses. They state the condition or modification of the main clause.

> s. conj.   dependent clause   independent clause
> "If *everything seems under control,* you're just not going fast enough."
> (race car driver Mario Andretti)

It is easy enough to recognize independent clauses, but **dependent clauses** can be harder to recognize, at first, because they can play so many roles. They often appear embedded in the sentence, and their subordinating conjunctions are not as easy to recognize as coordinating conjunctions. Words such as *what*, *that*, *how*, *which*, and *who*, referred to as *functional relatives*, often signal a dependent clause.

Hannah Arendt (1906–1975)

Arendt was born in Hanover, Germany, the only child of secular Jewish parents. As a student, she studied with Martin Heidegger and Karl Jaspers. In 1930 she married a Jewish philosopher and took up residence in Berlin; in 1933, after escaping the Gestapo, she and her husband fled to Paris. In 1939 they divorced, and in 1940 she married Heinrich Blücher, a German political refugee.

In 1941 Arendt was interned in Gurs, a concentration camp in southern France. but she escaped and fled

Oscar White/Corbis

to America, where she quickly became a part of an intellectual circle in New York City. She spent the next 30 years writing and teaching, becoming one of the most influential philosophers of the twentieth century. Arendt's political writings contain recurrent themes of "the inquiry into the conditions of possibility for a humane and democratic public life, the historical, social and economic forces that had come to threaten it, the conflictual relationship between private interests and the public good, [and] the impact of intensified cycles of production and consumption that destabilized the common world context of human life . . . ." (Majid Yar *Internet Encyclopedia of Philosophy*).

Dependent clause acting as subject:

subject clause   predicate   subject clause
"*Who controls the past* controls the future; *who controls the present*

predicate
controls the past." (George Orwell, *Nineteen Eighty-Four*)

Clause acting as sentence completion:

subject verb   sentence completion
"A person hears only *what they understand.*" (Johann Wolfgang von Goethe)

Here, *what* is the subordinating conjunction. However, *what* can also be the subject of a clause:

subject   s/v
"The hardest thing to see is *what is* in front of your eyes."
(Johann Wolfgang von Goethe)

That clauses are frequently used in essay writing. In a *that* clause, the relative *that* is the subordinating conjunction. *That* clauses act as subjects or completions, or appositives:

- Subject: *That the premise was correct* is arguable.
- Completion: She knows *that you are without blame.*
- Appositive: The idea *that he was telling the truth* was laughable.

An **appositive** restates the subject, modifying, expanding, describing.

Context

Arendt's quotation takes on more force when you know that she was a political philosopher who specialized in analyzing the rise of totalitarian regimes, in particular that of the Nazis in Germany. Given her life, it is not surprising that her first major work was *The Origins of Totalitarianism.* In 1961 she travelled to Jerusalem to cover the trial of Nazi Adolf Eichmann; she published her controversial reflections first in *The New Yorker* and then in book form.

In the *Internet Encyclopedia of Philosophy,* Majid Yar of Lancaster University helps elucidate Arendt's political views, as expressed in her controversial statements on "the banality of evil" in reference to Eichmann, chief architect and executor of Hitler's genocidal "final solution." Yar states:

> Arendt's book about the Eichmann trial . . . marks a shift in her concerns from the nature of political *action*, to a concern with the faculties that underpin it— the interrelated activities of *thinking* and *judging.*
>
> . . . As far as Arendt could discern, Eichmann came to his willing involvement with the program of genocide through a failure or absence of the faculties of sound thinking and judgement. From Eichmann's trial in Jerusalem . . . Arendt concluded that far from exhibiting a malevolent hatred of Jews which could have accounted psychologically for his participation in the Holocaust, Eichmann was an utterly innocuous individual. He operated unthinkingly, following orders, efficiently carrying them out, with no consideration of their effects upon those he targeted. . . .
>
> It was not the *presence* of hatred . . . but the *absence* of the imaginative capacities that would have made the human and moral dimensions of his activities tangible for him. Eichmann failed to exercise his capacity of *thinking*, of having an internal dialogue with himself, which would have permitted self-awareness of the evil nature of his deeds.

Discussion Questions

Recognizing clauses helps us to read and better understand complex sentences; for example, we recognize that we must separate the final *who* clause in Arendt's quotation at the beginning of this lesson, which suggests ideas for contemplation: Why don't people make up their minds to be good or evil? What prevents them?

Exercise

Write three sentences using a relative *that* clause—once as a subject, once as a completion, and once as an appositive. You might use the failure of thinking as the theme.

Suggested Readings

Eichmann in Jerusalem
The Origins of Totalitarianism

15 Martin Luther King Jr
Clauses

"The hottest place in Hell is reserved for those who remain neutral in times of great moral conflict."

To Review

✓ Identify the parts of speech, complete subject, finite verb, sentence completion, and clauses in King's quotation.

Clauses are complex, but they are not a mystery, and they can be identified and understood. There are two main questions to ask:

- *Is the clause dependent or independent?*

  Independent clauses stand on their own and are of equal value in the sentence; they are joined by a coordinating conjunction (*but, and, for, so, or,* etc.), a conjunctive adverb, parataxis, or correlative conjunctions (*if/then, either/or,* etc.).

  "If a man is called to be a street sweeper, [*then*] he should sweep streets even as Michelangelo painted, or Beethoven played music, or Shakespeare wrote poetry." (Martin Luther King Jr)

  Dependent clauses cannot stand alone and are joined by subordinating conjunctions, including functional relatives (*that, who, where, which,* etc.).

  "He should sweep streets so well that all the hosts of heaven and earth will pause to say, here lived a great street sweeper who did his job well." (Martin Luther King Jr)

- *What role does the clause play—is it a subject, object, or modifier?*

  "I am not interested in power for power's sake, but I'm interested in power that is moral, that is right and that is good." (Martin Luther King Jr)

  Here, the dependent *that* clauses modify *power.*

Look at the following quotation. We can identify three clauses:

s/v   s/v

"The ultimate measure of a man is not *where he stands in moments of*

Martin Luther King Jr (1929–1968)
Martin Luther King Jr, born in Atlanta, Georgia, was an outstanding student in public school, college, university, and divinity college. In his short lifetime, he received countless awards and honourary degrees, acknowledging his influence and his work in the civil rights movement. Ordained at 19 in the Baptist church, the third generation of pastors in his family, he was continually accosted, attacked, and arrested during his 13 years of struggle to raise consciousness about segregation, voting rights, intolerable working conditions, and other injustices toward African-Americans, in order to create change. King, a believer in Gandhi's form of non-violent protest, was a beacon of hope and inspiration, not only for the black community, but for people who wanted fairness and justice for all. At 33, he gave his famous "I have a dream" speech to 250,000 people in Washington, DC, which galvanized the country. At 35 he was the youngest man ever to receive the Nobel Peace Prize. He gave the prize money ($54,123) to help fund the civil rights movement. Tragically, at 39, he was assassinated in Memphis, Tennessee, by James Earl Ray.

World History Archive/ Alamy

King's legacy is still felt through his writing and his speeches. A powerful rhetorical speaker, King could move the masses, which was why he was so feared by those who wanted to maintain the status quo, who did not want change or fairness or justice for all, who wanted to maintain the cruel lie of white supremacy. King is remembered and revered as the symbolic leader of the American civil rights movement.

s/v
comfort and convenience,/but where he stands at times of challenge and controversy." (Martin Luther King Jr, *Strength to Love*)

In each case there is a subject/finite verb connection. At first glance the clauses appear to be independent because of the use of a correlative (*not/but*), but on closer scrutiny the use of *where* does not allow the clauses to stand on their own. Plus, the second and third clauses actually complete the main clause. The dependent clauses are acting as the completion of the subject: *the ultimate measure of a man* is not *this* but *that*. Remember that linking verbs such as *is* do not take objects.

The Greatest Sin

In Dante's *Inferno*, the deepest part of Hell is a frozen lake, Cocytus (Greek for "to lament"), reserved for Satan, a giant beast who is imprisoned, frozen mid-breast in the ice, in the ninth and last circle of Hell. The beast has three heads. Under each chin is a pair of bat-like wings that he beats, creating three cold winds, which continually freeze the ice surrounding him and those around him. Each of his three mouths chews eternally on the three other ultimate betrayers—Brutus, Cassius, and Judas.

For Dante, betrayal of one's benefactor is the greatest sin.

For psychologist Carl Jung, the greatest sin is to be unconscious.

For Martin Luther King Jr, the greatest sin is to remain neutral in times of great moral conflict.

Discussion Questions

- Why might neutrality be "a sin" in times of moral conflict?
- Can you think of times in history when people's choices to remain neutral caused harm or suffering?
- Are there situations today where we are either pretending ignorance or claiming neutrality to someone else's great harm?
- What do you consider to be the greatest sin?
- What makes the quotation at the beginning of this lesson memorable?

Exercises

Identify the main clauses in the two sentences below, and then identify the s/v connections, subordinate clause, and phrases. What part of speech do the phrases act as? (Hint: try substituting one word.) Distinguish the verbs from the auxiliaries and adverbs:

"Occasionally in life there are those moments of unutterable fulfillment which cannot be completely explained by those symbols called words. Their meanings can only be articulated by the inaudible language of the heart." (Martin Luther King Jr, Nobel Peace Prize acceptance lecture)

Suggested Reading

A Testament of Hope: The Essential Writings and Speeches of Martin Luther King Jr

16 Johann Wolfgang von Goethe
Punctuating Clauses, Restrictive and Non-restrictive Clauses

"First and last, what is demanded of genius is love of truth."

To Review
- ✓ Identify the subject and predicate in Goethe's quotation.
- ✓ Identify the two clauses and their subject/verb connections. What role does the subordinating clause play in the sentence?

Note: *first* and *last* are adverbs; here they are used in an **absolute phrase** modifying the whole sentence.

Conventions for Punctuating Clauses

As we learned in lesson 10, **independent clauses** can be joined in one of four ways:

- by a coordinating conjunction preceded by a comma:

  "Correction does much, but encouragement does more." (Johann Wolfgang von Goethe)

- by correlative conjunctions, separated by a comma:

  "Not only is there but one way of doing things rightly, but also there is only one way of seeing them rightly, and that is, seeing the whole of them." (John Ruskin, *The Two Paths*)

- by parataxis, using a semicolon:

  "Knowing is not enough; we must apply. Willing is not enough; we must do." (Johann Wolfgang von Goethe)

- by a conjunctive adverb (*however, in fact, therefore*), with a semicolon before and a comma after the adverb, although writers will sometimes drop the comma:

  "All you have shall some day be given; therefore give now, that the season of giving may be yours and not your inheritors'." (Kalib Gibran, *The Prophet*)

Classic Image/Alamy

Johann Wolfgang von Goethe (1749–1832)

Goethe—novelist, playwright, courtier, and natural philosopher—was born in Frankfurt, Germany. He was taught informally at home by his parents and tutors until he was 16, when he went to Leipzig University and later to Strasbourg and Frankfurt to study law. But from an early age, he was interested and involved in writing. His first novel, *The Sorrows of Young Werther* (1774), was highly acclaimed. His first dramatic success propelled him to the top of Germany's literary world. In 1775 he was invited to the court of Duke Karl August at Weimar and offered the title of privy councillor, creating a great scandal, as the position was traditionally held by a noble. The scandal intensified as Goethe became Duke August's closest friend, and they proceeded to break all the conventions of court. However, Goethe took good care of Duke August's affairs, as a council member, member of the war commission, director of roads, and financial manager of the court. He spent most of his life at Weimar, but he often travelled. In 1792 he left to fight against France in the French Revolution; when he returned, he worked as the manager of the court theatres until 1817.

Goethe's process was to work on his writing in his head until it was nearly polished, then write it down almost complete. He wrote his most famous play, *Faust*, across 57 years of his literary career, finally publishing it when he was 81. Throughout his life Goethe pursued a diversity of interests including aesthetics, botany, anatomy, and geology, to which he made several significant contributions.

Dependent clauses are subject to different rules. Punctuating dependent clauses depends on whether or not they are restrictive or non-restrictive.

This distinction often confuses, but really it is straightforward. The difference between the two is that **restrictive clauses**, as you might surmise from the name, do not take commas because the clause is part of the essential meaning—it cannot be separated or removed without fundamentally changing the meaning of the sentence. Say we wrote "*the maid who heard voices was burned at the stake*," referring to St. Joan. The restrictive clause *who heard voices* cannot be separated from the rest of the meaning. Not any maid was burned—the maid *who heard voices* was burned. So we don't separate it; we don't use commas.

Often, restrictive clauses interrupt the main clause:

Nothing *that can be taught* is worth teaching. (Oscar Wilde)

(This holds true for restrictive phrases as well.)

On the other hand, **non-restrictive clauses** do take commas because the information is not essential to the meaning; it is added information, relevant but not essential. In our case of St. Joan, we could write *"the maid, who became a saint, was called Joan of Arc."* Sainthood is not essential to the meaning, it is added information; it could be removed without changing the meaning of the main clause. Think of the commas as two hooks with which you could lift the clause out of the sentence without disturbing the rest.

This holds true for a non-restrictive *phrase*:

"Character, *in great and little things*, means carrying through what you feel able to do." (Johann Wolfgang von Goethe)

How do you know whether to use *that* or *which*? Remember this rule of thumb: restrictive clauses take *that*; non-restrictive clauses take *which*.

The Pursuit of Truth

Goethe is not alone in thinking that greatness is tied to the love of truth. The American education reformer, Horace Mann, once said, "seek not greatness, but seek truth and you will find both." The philosopher, Friedrich Nietzsche said, "on the mountains of truth you can never climb in vain: either you will reach a point higher up today, or you will be training your powers so that you will be able to climb higher tomorrow."

So how do we find truth? In ancient Greece, over the entrance to the Oracle of Delphi were the words "know thyself." This is not navel gazing; the Oracle's message implies critically examining your choices, assessing whether you have formed your own beliefs or just unknowingly adopted them along the way. Socrates said that the unexamined life is not worth living. The Oracle implied that the seekers would have to use their own self-knowledge to unravel her cryptic answers. This is the process of understanding. We will not discover truth by merely listening to others, jumping on bandwagons, or believing everything we hear. Nor is accumulating information the same as understanding. Knowledge comes from study, weaving together information in our own way, with the help of the best thinkers we can find; it is a process of absorbing, critically assessing, examining all sides, selecting, drawing our own conclusions. And we cannot approach truth from our head only; we must also engage our heart.

Discussion Questions

- What parts of your life are unexamined?
- What beliefs do you hold that you have never actually examined?
- What other absolute phrase could Goethe have used in his quotation?
- How can we find truth in our time, when we are daily bombarded with every manner of persuasive advertising, political doublespeak, and pseudo mythologies?

Exercise

Review quotations at the beginning of lessons 10–13 and examine the use of punctuation for clauses. Has the writer followed or broken the convention? If broken, to what effect?

Suggested Readings

The Sorrows of Young Werther
Faust
From My Life: Poetry and Truth

17 David Suzuki
Compound-Complex Sentences, Analogies

"We're in a giant car heading towards a brick wall, and everyone's arguing over where they're going to sit."

To Review

✓ Identify the dependent and independent clauses in Suzuki's quotation.

A **compound-complex sentence** has at least two independent clauses (making it compound), and at least one dependent clause (making it complex). It can be long and complicated; thus, it is imperative that you, as a writer, adhere strictly to precise grammatical patterns. By following a few rules, you will keep your compound-complex sentences clear:

1. Use the conventions for punctuating clauses (see lesson 16). **Punctuation** separates elements to make the meaning clear to the reader.

2. When describing or explaining, present events in the order in which they occur. In *The Writing Life*, Annie Dillard not only explains what to do when you know there is a fatal flaw in your essay, but also provides a model for the ordering rule:

   "What do you do? Acknowledge, first, that you cannot do nothing. Lay out the structure you already have, x-ray it for a hairline fracture, find it, and think about it for a week or a year; solve the insoluble problem."

   Note how Dillard uses parallel imperative verbs (*acknowledge, lay, x-ray, find, think, solve*) to enhance the clarity of her explanation.

3. Use **parallel constructions** (repetition of an exact grammatical structure).

   "Some cause happiness wherever they go; others, whenever they go." (Oscar Wilde)

   Note the **ellipsis** before the subordinate clause signalled by the comma in Wilde's quotation: "*others, (cause happiness) whenever they go.*" An ellipsis refers to any deliberate grammatical omission in the structure of the sentence

David Suzuki (b. 1936)
David Suzuki is probably best known as the inspiring host of CBC Television's *The Nature of Things*. He has dedicated his life to educating Canadians about environmental issues. His goals have been constant—to help preserve the natural world for future generations and to develop sustainability in our lifetime.

His personal history is also inspiring. He was born in Vancouver in 1936; during World War II he spent formative years of his young life in an internment camp. At the end of the war, stripped of their former life, his family was relocated to Ontario. A man of extraordinary vision, Suzuki went on to become a renowned geneticist, author of more than 30 books, and Canada's most famous scientific spokesperson. In 1990, he founded the David Suzuki Foundation, a non-profit organization dedicated to finding innovative ways to help conserve the natural world. A Companion of the Order of Canada, he has been honoured with many awards and distinctions.

David Suzuki Foundation

4.   Choose your conjunction carefully. Conjunctives establish relationships such as time (*meanwhile, lately*), space (*beyond, above*), or logic (*therefore, because*). You want to vary the conjunctions you use, but use them precisely. In argument, you should not repeatedly use *therefore*, nor should you use *thus* if you haven't made the connection explicit. A conjunction cannot do the work of argument, it can only connect.

There are basically four ways to punctuate a series, whether it consists of words, phrases, or clauses:

- commas and one conjunction: *foes, friends, and lovers*
- commas only: *foes, friends, lovers*
- conjunctions only: *foes and friends and lovers*
- commas and multiple conjunctions: *foes, and friends, and lovers*

(A fifth way involves an extra phrase set off by a comma; in this case, you would use semicolons to separate the elements: *foes, who break you; friends; and lovers*.) Read each example out loud to hear the rhythmic effect.

Analogy
Suzuki's quotation is an **analogy**—a writing device worth developing. Analogy is akin to simile and metaphor; it too provides a comparison. An analogy yokes together two unlike things in order to highlight some point or points of similarity. Analogy is used in both creative and argumentative writing, often

to make an unfamiliar concept more relatable. As Freud said, "Analogies prove nothing that is quite true, but they can make one feel more at home" (90). Good writers use them. They are most commonly constructed in a few sentences, but may structure an entire comparative essay.

If you find Suzuki's use of analogy interesting, you might also enjoy Jim Merkel's *Radical Simplicity: Small Footprints on a Finite Earth*. In this book, Merkel uses a provocative analogy to raise ethical questions about environmental issues. Imagine, Merkel says, that you are first in line at a potluck buffet. The spread includes not just food and water, but all the materials needed for shelter, clothing, health care, and education. How do you know how much to take? How much is enough to leave for your neighbours behind you—not just the six billion people, but the wildlife, and those yet unborn? What if you were hidden behind a curtain—would your decision change?

Discussion Questions

- What is the comparison in Suzuki's quotation? What is the car implicitly compared to? Who's in the car? What is the brick wall implicitly compared to? What are we arguing about?
- Given what we know about Suzuki, what are the political and economic issues he's raising? In his view, what should we be focusing on? Why? Do you agree?

Exercises

1. Identify the clauses in the following quotation:

   "If children grow up understanding that we are animals, they will look at other species with a sense of fellowship and community. If they understand their ecological place—the biosphere—then when children see the great virgin forests of the Queen Charlotte Islands being clearcut, they will feel physical pain, because they will understand that those trees are an extension of themselves." (David Suzuki, *Inventing the Future*)

   Do you agree with Suzuki's choice of punctuation?
2. Describe your home street using a single sentence. Concentrate on ensuring a coherent order and choosing the correct conjunction(s). Try using a parallel construction.

Suggested Readings

The Sacred Balance: Rediscovering Our Place in Nature
The David Suzuki Reader

18 Barbara Gowdy
Fragments, Pronouns, Tone

"My memory is photographic, in living colour. I'm flooded with memories, mostly images from dreams I've had. A leather jacket with four tulips, eating blueberries half blind and having blueberries scattered on the ground, growing limbs that turn out to be tree limbs, useless." ("The Two-Headed Man," in We So Seldom Look on Love)

To Review
✓ Identify the parts of speech and subject/verb connections in Gowdy's quotation.

Fragments

Along with the other sentences we have been examining, there is one other kind that writers use: a **fragment**. This type of sentence is incomplete, usually because it lacks a verb, but sometimes because the subject has been dropped even though it is not meant as an imperative. A fragment is often used to enliven writing by approximating the staccato style of conversation, or disjunctive fragments of thought. However, *Fowler's Modern English Usage* lists six other uses: transitional, afterthought, dramatic climax, comment, pictorial, and aggressive (674–5).

WARNING: Most professors consider fragments to be grammatical errors. Most errors occur when writers use verbals instead of verbs, believing they are writing complete sentences. Note the third sentence in Gowdy's quotation; it has lots of verbals—*eating, having, scattered, growing, to be*—but no finite verb. Nor is the leather jacket the true subject of that sentence. This third sentence is a list; conventionally, we would use a colon instead of the period at the end of the second sentence. Why do you think Gowdy chose not to? Skilled writers such as Gowdy use the fragment not only for the reasons listed above, but also for emphasis, variety, and rhythm. Most use it sparingly. A few fiction writers use it frequently as part of their distinct style—for example, Sheila Watson and James Joyce. Consider the following example from *Ulysses*:

—Will you tell him he can kiss my arse? Myles Crawford said, throwing out his arm for emphasis. Tell him that straight from the stable.

Barbara Gowdy (b. 1950)
Born in Windsor, Ontario, and raised in Toronto, Gowdy has been an editor and a part-time creative writing lecturer, but she is best known as a writer of unique novels and unsettling short stories. Her characters are abnormal in the extreme—a necrophiliac; a four-legged woman; Siamese twins; a two-headed man with, of course, two minds. One would expect these stories to be shocking and sensational, but Gowdy chronicles these unconventional lives with such compassion that the reader is drawn into the characters' worlds to experience their fantastic and heart-breaking lives. We are shown with unsentimental clarity the most unusual relationships, families, desires, and passions, until our moral ground quakes and then moves.

Geraint Lewis/Alamy

Gowdy has read her works in Canada, the United States, and throughout Great Britain, and given on-air readings for Danish and American radio stations. A number of her stories have been made into movies.

A bit nervy. Look out for squalls. All off for a drink. Arm in arm. Lenehan's yachting cap on the cadge beyond. Usual blarney. Wonder is that young Dedalus the moving spirit. Has a good pair of boots on him today. Last time I saw him he had his heels on view. Been walking in muck somewhere. Careless chap. What was he doing in Irishtown?

Pronouns

There are three basic forms of **pronouns**: subject form (*I, you, he, she, it, we, they*), object form (*me, you, him, her, it, us, them*), and possessive form (*my/ mine, your/yours, his, her/hers, its, our/ours, their/theirs*). A pronoun takes the place of a noun (its antecedent or referent—what it refers to). A pronoun must appear near its antecedent. Whenever possible, the antecedent should precede the pronoun. If you use more than one pronoun in a sentence, make sure the antecedents are clear. The pronoun must agree with its referent in person, number, and gender.

ant. 1   pro. 1 ant. 2 pro. 1
"Many people take no care of *their* money till *they* come nearly to the end
pro. 2 ant. 3   pro. 3
of *it*, and others do just the same with *their* time." (Johann Wolfgang von Goethe)

The first antecedent, *people*, is in the third person, a mass noun treated as plural, and gender neutral—hence the use of *their* and *they*; the second antecedent is *money*, which is a mass noun treated as singular and also gender neutral—hence the use of *it*. The third antecedent, *others*, (a noun substituting for "other people") is in the third person, plural, and gender neutral—hence the use of *their*.

Tone

When we refer to a writer's **tone**, we generally mean the writer's (or literary speaker's) attitude toward his or her reader. A tone can be subjective or objective, ironic or matter-of-fact, serious or playful, arrogant or humble, and so on.

Why is tone important, and why should you—the writer—choose your tone carefully? Think of tone as expressing your voice. M.H. Abrams states that "the way we speak reveals, by subtle clues, our conception of, and attitude to, the things we are talking about, our personal relationship to our auditor, and also our assumptions about the social level, intelligence, and sensitivity of that auditor" (218). We pick up those clues quickly, and what holds true in speech, holds true in writing.

Examine Gowdy's tone in the quotation at the beginning of this lesson. Like Atwood and Marquez, Gowdy uses a detached, objective, matter-of-fact tone to help her readers suspend their disbelief of her unusual ideas:

> Merry Mary is referring to the fact that Sylvie's Siamese twin, Sue, is attached to her. Sue is nothing but a pair of legs, though. Perfect little legs, with feet, knees, thighs, hips and a belly, just under her own navel, and the feet hanging to a few inches below her own knees and facing away from her body; that is to say, facing in the same direction as her own feet. ("Sylvia," in *We So Seldom Look on Love*)

Like Marquez, Gowdy mixes realism and the fantastic, treating the extraordinary as if it were ordinary.

Discussion Questions

- What tone(s) of voice do you dislike?
- In argument, what tone persuades you most readily?
- Describe the tone of your favourite academic writer.

Exercise

Write a paragraph in a tone you have never explored in writing. Once you have chosen your tone, choose a topic to suit the tone. (Of course, generally we do this the other way around!)

Suggested Readings

We So Seldom Look On Love
The White Bone
Mister Sandman

19 **Angela Carter**
Interruption, Allusion

"Aeneas carried his aged father on his back from the ruins of Troy and so do we all, whether we like it or not, perhaps even if we have never known them." (Virago Book of Fairy Tales)

To Review
✓ How many clauses are there in Carter's quotation? How many are subordinate?
✓ What kind of a sentence is this?
✓ What kind of conjunction is *even if*?
✓ Where might Carter have put another comma?

Another device used for emphasis is **interruption**. An interruption is a word, phrase, or clause that splits apart the main clause in a sentence. Like all emphatic devices, it must be used sparingly or it loses its effect and just ends up annoying your reader. But used prudently, it catches the reader's attention and throws emphasis on the interruption itself, what follows, or both.

A single word is the least disruptive interruption:

"It is, perhaps, better to be valued as an object of passion than never to be valued at all." (Angela Carter, "A Souvenir of Japan," in *Fireworks: Nine Profane Pieces*)

The word *perhaps* suggests to the reader that Carter is not being entirely serious—this quotation is, after all, a parody of Alfred Lord Tennyson's line from "In Memoriam": "'Tis better to have loved and lost than never to have loved at all.'

A phrase provides a more distinct break. Note in the following quotation how the interjection not only emphasizes itself, but also enhances the effect of this periodic sentence—we don't know the full meaning of the sentence until we come to the very last word:

"When you have eliminated the impossible, whatever remains, *however improbable*, must be the truth." (Sir Arthur Conan Doyle, *The Sign of the Four*)

An interrupting clause is the most disruptive interruption. In lesson 13 we examined three positions in which to put a main clause in a complex sentence: beginning, middle, or end. A fourth position, in which a lesser clause interrupts the main clause, is called a convoluted sentence. In academic writing, this often involves appositives:

Interfoto/Alamy

Angela Carter (1940–1992)
Angela Carter, British novelist, short story writer, and cultural journalist, was born in Sussex in the middle of World War II , and was shortly evacuated to Yorkshire to live with her maternal grandmother. She left school at 19 to work on the *Croydon Advertiser*, a London-area newspaper, later studying English at the University of Bristol. She married, but 12 years later, just after winning the Somerset Maugham Award for literature, she divorced and moved to Japan. She travelled widely, wrote profusely—novels, short stories, fairy tales, reviews. In 1977, she remarried and settled in London, and for 10 years taught at numerous universities. She died at the age of 51 from cancer, at the height of her writing life.

Linden Peach, from the University of Gloucestershire, calls Carter "An exemplary 'postmodern', [whose] novels and stories stand almost without parallel in British writing for their complex blending of parody, allegory and symbolism and their generic mixing of fantasy, romance, the gothic and science fiction." Her unique novels draw on forms including "the fairy story, the folk tale and myth, on the picaresque mode of seventeenth- and eighteenth-century fiction, and the more popular forms of theatre such as the musical and the pantomime." In a tribute, 14 years after Carter's death, Roz Kaveney described her as "the poet of the urban jungle, as well as of the wild wood where we find danger, and the haunted palaces of love where vampires lurk"; a writer whose tales are full of powerful images: "werewolves and harlequins, drag queens and jewelled flowers, stopped clocks and sharp blades."

The real Macbeth, *who ruled Alba for 17 years*, was nothing like the murderous character Shakespeare created, at least, not for his time.

In interjection, *the main clause* is interrupted. Decide if this is true for the following quotation:

"Strangers used to gather together at the cinema and sit together in the dark, like Ancient Greeks participating in the mysteries, dreaming the same dream in unison." (Angela Carter)

Notice the punctuation in all of the examples of interjection above. It is almost too good to be true—a rule with no exceptions? Do interjections always take commas? Well, almost. An unrestrictive interjection requires commas around it. A restrictive interjection does not:

The bell *lying on the table* rang inexplicably.

It was not any bell that rang—only the one lying on the table.

Allusion

In order to understand the comparison Carter draws, we need to answer two questions: *who was Aeneas?* and *what were the ruins of Troy?* This reference reveals the joy of allusion. Allusion is a passing reference, without explicit explanation, to something that is considered well-known, something shared between writer and reader: usually a literary, mythical, or historical figure, place, or event. Either we get it, or we don't, so one should always make the effort to discover the allusion's meaning. Unquestionably, it is adding layers of meaning. You, indubitably, will come across that same allusion again. Writers use allusion because it is efficient—you can allude to a character, event or whole work in a few words, efficiently illustrating or expanding your subject.

The Trojan War is a rich source for allusion. It is a complex story encompassing many characters you may have heard of—Paris, Helen, Agamemnon, Odysseus, Achilles, Aeneas—even if you have not read Greek mythology. In short, a thousand Spartan ships set sail for Troy to reclaim Helen, the wife of Menelaus stolen by Paris of Troy; they besiege the city for ten years. Eventually, the Greeks invade the city by way of a gift—a large, hollow, wooden horse secretly filled with Greek soldiers who attack Troy that night, forcing the Trojans to flee. Aeneas, a Trojan prince, physically carries his aged father, Anchises, from the burning ruins and leads the surviving Trojans to a new home in Italy.

It is worth reading the Greek myths because Western culture is saturated with allusions referring to them.

Discussion Questions

In Carter's quotation at the beginning of this lesson, she uses Aeneas's physical act to metaphorically illustrate the mental act of carrying familial baggage. Why do we carry this baggage "even if we have never known them"? Is it because of stories told, genetics, obsession with the unknown? Do you agree? Should we carry this baggage? (As an aside, R.D. Laing, in *The Politics of the Family*, has some interesting things to say on this and related topics.)

Exercise

Write three sentences, perhaps on the theme of familial obligation. In the first sentence, use one word to interrupt a main clause; in the second, use an interrupting phrase; and in the third, use an interrupting clause.

Suggested Readings

Nights at the Circus
Expletives Deleted: Selected Writings
Greek Mythology by Robert Graves
Mythology by Edith Hamilton

20 A Cornucopia of Voices
Figures of Speech: Metaphor, Simile

Understanding figures of speech is often the bane of a student's existence—especially when studying poetry. If you believe that the poet or writer is trying to hide something from you, trying to be difficult, you miss the point and joy of metaphorical language. As a method of understanding figures of speech, Simone Weil suggests "not to try to interpret them, but to look at them until the light suddenly dawns" (109). It begins with what T.S. Eliot called "auditory imagination"; the idea that language (even a foreign language) heard *before* we understand it will elicit a response (Schmidt 672). Perhaps we just have to trust that response. Figurative language allows us to use something familiar to evoke, describe, or explain something unfamiliar. Metaphor and simile compare two things that are unalike, but that have something significant in common.

Remember what we learned in lesson 3:

metaphor = *tenor* (subject) + <u>vehicle</u> (expression)

Metaphor:

"*The Falklands thing* was <u>a fight between two bald men over a comb</u>."
(J.L. Borges, "On the Falklands War," editorial, *Time magazine*)

"When you write you lay out a line of words. The line of words is a miner's pick, a woodcarver's gouge, a surgeon's probe." (Annie Dillard, *The Writing Life*)

"A riot is at bottom the language of the unheard." (Martin Luther King Jr, *Chaos or Community*)

"Life is a sexually transmitted disease and the mortality rate is one hundred per cent." (R.D. Laing)

A **simile** is also made up of a tenor and a vehicle, often linked by *like* or *as*:

"He looked about as inconspicuous as a tarantula on a slice of angel food." (Raymond Chandler, *Farewell, My Lovely*)

"Venice is like eating an entire box of chocolate liqueurs in one go." (Truman Capote)

"Life is like an onion: You peel it off one layer at a time, and sometimes you weep." (Carl Sandburg)

"To choose doubt as a philosophy of life is akin to choosing immobility as a means of transportation." (Yann Martel, *Life of Pi*)

A metaphor is an implied comparison, whereas a simile is a direct comparison. F.L. Lucas describes the difference: "the simile sets two ideas side by side; in the metaphor they become superimposed."

Discussion Questions

Let's take a closer look at metaphor, which can often be more difficult to interpret than simile. In the following quotation, Goethe superimposes his ideas, with the added complexity of an ellipsis:

"He who cannot draw on three thousand years is living from hand to mouth."

The quotation raises two questions: Three thousand years of what? What does Goethe mean by "hand to mouth"? We know the expression means "in poverty"—eating meagrely whatever is at hand. However, Goethe cannot be talking about food. What is he talking about? There are a number of issues he could be referring to, and not all of them involve reading, but we might interpret one as illiteracy. A more tragic tale would be that of one who *can* read but chooses not to use this skill to gain the accumulated wisdom of our past. Surely, one who does not know of myths, or songs, or stories, or history, or scientific discoveries, or philosophic truths is living "hand to mouth"—a meagre, impoverished existence. How do you interpret the quotation?

Exercises

1. Identify the tenor and the vehicle in the metaphors and similes presented in the lesson.
2. Construct your own similes using the examples from the lesson as models:

   Toronto is like _____. Life is like a _____.

3. Next, turn your similes into metaphors.

Suggested Readings

Jan Zwicky, *Wisdom and Metaphor*
Robert Scholes, et al., *Text Book: An Introduction to Literary Language*

21 A Plethora of Voices
Emphatic Devices: Repetition

The rhetorical use of **repetition** is a powerful device for any writer. For strong examples from oration, we just have to think of the political speeches of Pierre Elliott Trudeau or Barack Obama, but repetition can be an equally powerful tool for the writer when used judiciously and to emphasize ideas of significance. Three types of effective repetition are **parallel construction**, syntactic patterning, and patterns of repetition. You will find that these often overlap.

In parallel construction, the writer repeats an exact grammatical pattern. This construction is often formed using parataxis:

> "Hatred paralyzes life; love releases it. Hatred confuses life; love harmonizes it. Hatred darkens life; love illuminates it." (Martin Luther King Jr, *Strength to Love*)

Note that King uses not only a parallel construction (noun verb noun, noun verb pronoun) but also a pattern of repetition (*hatred/life*; *love/it*).

Parallel constructions also frequently consist of repeated **prepositional phrases**:

> "In every outthrust headland, in every curving beach, in every grain of sand there is a story of the earth." (Rachel Carson, "Our Ever-Changing Shore," in *Holiday* magazine)

Note how the suspense builds not only with the use of repetition, but also with the reader's anticipation of the main idea, which is kept to the very end.

In syntactic patterning, the writer repeats a basic structure in successive sentences or clauses:

> "Time is the substance from which I am made. Time is a river which carries me along, but I am the river; it is a tiger that devours me, but I am the tiger; it is a fire that consumes me, but I am the fire." (Jorge Luis Borges, "A New Refutation of Time" in *Other Inquisitions 1937–1952*)

Note that the use of rhythm, metaphor, and patterns of repetition also enhance the textual power.

Syntactic patterns can also be formed by using the conjunction *and*:

"The notion of a universality of human experience is a confidence trick and the notion of a universality of female experience is a clever confidence trick." (Angela Carter, *The Sadeian Woman*)

Imagine this quotation using parataxis—does the meaning change? I would argue that the conjunction is more inclusive. Parataxis would separate the female experience from the human experience in a way that Carter would not have wanted. The semicolon is a stop, whereas the conjunction is a connection. Note that Carter does not even use a comma before the conjunction—a comma would suggest an unwanted pause.

Discussion Questions

There are numerous patterns of repetition first described by the Greeks, as you can surmise from their names, and a good writer will study them. Let's look briefly at a few. Remember that the repetition is used to emphasize a significant idea. How might you use these in an essay effectively? Invent your own example for each one. Which pattern do you find most effective for essay writing? Why?

Tautotes is the repetition of a word two or more times:

"Tomorrow and tomorrow and tomorrow / Creeps in this petty pace from day to day . . . ." (William Shakespeare, "Macbeth")

Diacope occurs when two identical words are separated by one or two words:

"It seemed incredible that this day, a day without warnings or omens, might be that of my implacable death." (Jorge Luis Borges, "The Garden of Forking Paths" [see also *El jardín de senderos que se bifurca*])

Anaphora is the repetition of a word at the beginning of successive phrases or clauses:

"From this youngest son's failure to dog-paddle the father saw other failures multiply like an explosion of virulent cells—failure to speak clearly; failure to sit up straight; failure to get up in the morning; failure of attitude; failure of ambition and ability; indeed, in everything. His own failure." (Annie Proulx, *The Shipping News*)

Epistrophe occurs when the same word ends successive phrases or clauses:

It is rather for us to be here dedicated to the great task remaining before us— that from these honoured dead we take increased devotion to that cause for which they here gave the last full measure of devotion—that we here highly resolve that these dead shall not have died in vain—that this nation, under God, shall have a new birth of freedom—and that government of the people, by the people, for the people, shall not perish from the earth. (Abraham Lincoln, "The Gettysburg Address")

Exercises

1. Using Borges's, Proulx's, and Carson's grammatical forms, write your own sentences.
2. In your next essay, try using one of the patterns of repetition to emphasis your most important idea.

22 George Elliott Clarke
Emphatic Devices: Accumulation

Black Madonna! I love your African essence, your faith in children, your insatiable desire for freedom, your swift intelligence, your sharp passion, your secret strengths, your language that tells no lies, your fashion that is colour, your music that is gospel-lullaby, your lips like crimson berries, your skin like soft, moist night, your eyes like dusk, your hair like dark cotton, your scent like rich butter, your taste like raisins and dates and sweet wine. (Whylah Falls)

To Review
✓ Identify patterns of repetition in Clarke's quotation.

There are basically three ways that you can draw attention to an idea in writing: (1) by using an emphatic sentence, such as a short, simple sentence, a freight train, or a periodic sentence; (2) by using emphatic devices *within* the sentence; and (3) by adding mechanical emphasis, which includes the use of exclamation marks, underlining, and capital letters. As exemplified in the beginning fragment of Clarke's quotation, this third method can play a dramatic role.

However, mechanical emphasis is less effective in formal writing, as in an essay. When you want to emphasize an idea within a sentence, there are other ways to do this, such as positioning the word you wish to highlight at the beginning or end of the sentence, or by using emphatic devices such as repetition, parallel construction, interruption, or accumulation.

Accumulation is the piling up of grammatical patterns. In the quotation at the beginning of this lesson, Clarke uses accumulation to emphasize the narrator's love for a woman—he compiles details that describe the beloved, giving the reader a full understanding of both the woman and what she means to the narrator. We can accumulate single words, phrases, or clauses. The following examples are profuse in their accumulation, but even a pairing of adjectives can be emphatic.

Examine the accumulation of *single words* (prepositions and adjectives) in the following quotation from James Joyce's *A Portrait of the Artist as a Young Man*:

> "The artist, like the God of the creation, remains within or behind or beyond or above his handiwork, invisible, refined out of existence, indifferent, paring his fingernails."

George Elliott Clarke (b. 1960)
George Elliott Clarke, born near Windsor Plains, Nova Scotia and raised in Halifax, is a seventh-generation African-Canadian. He has made many contributions to Canadian culture and society—as an editor, publisher, social worker, researcher, journalist, academic, screen-writer, critic, parliamentary aide, and most recently as Toronto's fourth poet laureate—but he is best known as a poet, playwright, and novelist. A gifted poet,

Elizabeth Eve/Writers'   Clarke has written seven books of poetry in his sensual,
Federation of Nova Scotia   sinuous, rhythmic, lush, lyrical style. As Clarke said,
"I craved to draft lyrics that would pour out like pentecostal fire—pell mell, scorching, bright, loud: a poetics of arson."

His novel, *George & Rue*, the story of a "slug-ugly crime," is in the order that Franz Kafka described when he said books should "bite and sting us." It tells the story of two of Clarke's first cousins, who in 1949 hammered to death a taxi-driver, stole his money, ditched him, and were later hanged for their crimes. It also tells the story of unrelenting poverty in a black community in the back-woods of New Brunswick. Clarke, an Officer of the Order of Canada, first told this story in his Governor General's Award-winning collection, *Execution Poems*.

Note how Joyce uses accumulation to expand a basic sentence: *The artist remains invisible behind his handiwork*. What is the effect of the accumulation of prepositions and modifiers?

The accumulation of *phrases and clauses* can have a more complex effect, emphasizing and expanding the writer's original point, as demonstrated in the following quotation from Jeanette Winterson's *Art & Lies*:

> The spirit has gone out of the world. I fear the dead bodies settling around me, the corpses of humanity, fly-blown and ragged. I fear the executive zom-bies, the shop zombies, the Church zombies, the writerly zombies, all mouthing platitudes, the language of the dead, all mistaking hobbies for passions, the folly of the dead.

Patterns of repetition are often involved in accumulation. Note Winterson's use of anaphora (*I fear*); her repetition of *zombies* as the adjectives pile up; her accumulation of prepositional (*of the dead*) and participle (*mouthing plati-tudes/mistaking hobbies*) phrases.

Poetic Devices in Prose

Accumulation does not have to be profuse—subtle use can also be effective. In *Whylah Falls*, Clarke often pairs adjectives ("the *lean, livid* engine plunges through the night") or nouns ("Desire illuminates the dark manuscript of our skin with *beetles and butterflies*"). In both examples, alliteration helps to draw attention to the pairing, and metaphorical language increases the textual power. Together, the three devices produce a powerful effect. You might think, mistakenly, that these devices are effective only in poetry, but poetic language can be used to enhance all writing—it adds immeasurably to the reader's pleasure.

Clarke's academic style is more intense than most of us could handle, but his poetic devices infuse exuberant energy into the writing. In an article for the *Journal of Canadian Studies*, Clarke criticizes an opinion piece in *The Globe and Mail* about the state of African-Canadian literature, stating:

> Even carpal-tunnel-syndrome-challenged typists who jet newspapery opinions should attempt a minimal degree of scholarly probity, so as to prevent their inventing idiocies or venting idiosyncrasies.
>
> . . .
>
> [T]hose who insist upon a critique of African-Canadian literature that is more than either chauvinistic cheerleading or belles lettristic belligerence must constantly demand an adherence to scholarly principles. This precept means acknowledging that African Canada and its cultures constitute a rainbow of ethnicities and an opera of accents. It also means doing the hard but eminently respectable work of retrieving lost writers and excavating long-buried archives.
>
> It's *our* responsibility.

In your essay writing, pay attention to your choice of verbs—careful selection can add energy (as in Clarke's choice of *jet*). The next time you write an essay, try using *one* alliteration of paired adjectives or a piling up of adjectives or a metaphor (*an opera of accents*). The knack is to use these devices sparingly in places where you need to draw the reader's full attention.

Discussion Questions

- Clarke's quotation at the beginning of this lesson reveals his poetic eye for detail, his talent for using concrete images to make the "Black Madonna" come alive for the reader. Can you reduce this sentence and still retain its essence?
- What is the effect on the reader?
- What is lost?

Exercises

1. Describe someone or something you love, using an accumulation of single words. It does not have to be a beloved; it could be a family member, a friend, or a place.
2. Describe a fear using accumulation, but this time use phrases and/or clauses.

3. Use Joyce's grammatical pattern to write your own sentence defining a role such as that of the artist. For example, you could focus on the student, the professor, the athlete, the performer, or the friend.

Suggested Readings

Whylah Falls
George & Rue
Trudeau: Long March, Shining Path

23 Simone Weil
Emphatic Devices: Rhythm

"Even if our efforts of attention seem for years to be producing no result, one day a light that is in exact proportion to them will flood the soul."

To Review
- ✓ Identify the clauses, their subjects, finite verbs, and any verbals, conjunctives, or relative pronouns in Weil's quotation.
- ✓ What does the *that* clause modify? Is it restrictive or non-restrictive?

Reread Weil's quotation out loud until you hear its **rhythm**. A good writer, like a good composer, must have a good ear. Some writers have "perfect pitch." Many of the quotations we have studied are excellent examples of a writer's subtle but effective use of rhythm. We will look more thoroughly at rhythm in the longer excerpts in the lessons to come, but here are a few preliminary suggestions for enhancing the rhythm of your writing.

Get in the habit of reading your work out loud. Yes, even prose. Yes, even your essay for history or biology. Better still, get someone else to read it to you. You will hear any awkwardness, gaps, wordiness, and other failings that you don't always see when you are writing, and you will begin to hear the rhythms of your own distinct style.

Gustav Flaubert, a French writer, expressed the longing for perfection in eloquence this way:

> "Human speech is like a cracked kettle on which we tap crude rhythms for bears to dance to, while we long to make music that will melt the stars." (*Madame Bovary*)

Rhythm is not as easy to recognize as finite verbs or restrictive clauses; it is hard to point to, but that does not mean it is a frill, to be largely ignored. Rhythm will be present whether you pay attention to it or not, and your best ideas will fall flat if your rhythm is poor; so, make it work for you, not against you. Effective rhythm in formal writing is unobtrusive, working at a subconscious level for the reader. *Don't overdo it.*

Rhythm consists of stressed and unstressed syllables; effective rhythm pleases the ear, and by its own structure helps reinforce the writer's idea or feeling. Rhythm involves variation—for example, slowing down a periodic

Simone Weil (1909–1943)
Born in Paris, Simone Weil was a labour worker and organizer, resistance fighter (she was a member of the French Resistance during World War II), mystic, and philosopher. Weil's genius manifested itself early. At 15 she took her baccalauréat in philosophy. She was admitted into the prestigious École Normale Supérieure, where she was one of its first female students. Her short life was a bright flare of nonconformist intellectual pursuit. Susan Sontag described her as a "person who is excruciatingly identical with her ideas, the person who is rightly regarded as one of the most uncompromising and troubling witnesses to the modern travail of the spirit." Her Plato-inspired ethics included a rejection of force, and an uncompromising ascetic self-denial. She died at 34 of a lung condition complicated by self-imposed starvation, an act of protest against the suffering caused by Nazi forces. G.L. Arnold said she was "a spirit in whom the flame of resistance burned until the body wasted away. Antigone in modern dress." She left a body of writing—in the form of letters, diaries, essays, and articles—that is honest, brilliant, diverse, and controversial.

Interfoto/Alamy

sentence with two or three heavy beats or stressed syllables to make it *sound* like an ending. In Weil's quotation, note how the stressed accents on *flood* and *soul* slow the rhythm of the sentence.

You can vary the rhythm within a sentence or within a paragraph. A short, simple sentence in the midst of many long sentences varies the rhythm of the paragraph and, by so doing, draws attention to itself:

> "Do not allow yourself to be imprisoned by any affection. Keep your solitude. The day, if it ever comes, when you are given true affection there will be no opposition between interior solitude and friendship, quite the reverse. It is even by this infallible sign that you will recognize it." (Simone Weil, "Love," in *Gravity and Grace*)

Meaning in Metaphor

The quotation at the beginning of this lesson holds many subtleties. How might we approach Weil's meaning? The following passage from Weil's *American Diaries* helps to clarify her meaning:

> The authentic and pure values of the true, the beautiful, and the good in the activity of a human being are produced by way of a single act, a concentration upon an object in the fullness of one's attention . . . . This true attention consists of suspending our thought, leaving it detached, empty, and ready to be

penetrated by the object; it means holding in our minds, within reach of this thought, but on a lower level and not in contact with it, the diverse knowledge we have acquired which we are forced to make use of. Our thought should be in relation to all particular and already formulated thoughts, as a man on a mountain who, as he looks forward, sees also below him, without actually looking at them, a great many forests and plains." (qtd in Glenn)

Discussion Questions

Weil's meaning may be expressed in an image of a small child playing organized baseball and positioned in right field: crouched, hand on knee, glove ready, suspended in an empty green expanse but watching the infield intently—even though we all know that at this age, no ball ever makes it out to right field. This effort of attention, which seems to be producing no result, is teaching the child endurance, perseverance, and the very act of attention that will serve her well in years to come. In our world of instantaneous gratification, it is a lesson not easily acquired. This "true attention" may be connected to another idea attributed to Hippocrates and translated by Chaucer in *The Parliament of Fowles*: "The lyfe so short; the craft so long to lerne." How would you make the connection?

Weil's meaning in the quotation from *American Diaries* is enhanced by her use of rhythm. For example, she uses patterns of twos and threes: *The authentic and pure values; the true, the beautiful, and the good; suspending our thought, leaving it detached; forests and plains*. Consider the writers we have already examined. Whose style is most similar to Weil's?

Exercises

1. To achieve effective rhythm, the best practice is to read good writers out loud. Read Dickens, Dillard, Weil. Read any writer whose rhythm appeals to you and spend some time examining how he or she does it.
2. The next time you write an essay, attend to rhythm in your revision process. Read your work out loud, listening for its cadence. Start slowly, perhaps with your conclusion. Using a variety of sentence lengths and stressing the final syllables, make it *sound* like an ending.

Suggested Readings

Formative Writings, 1929–1941
American Diaries

24 The Canadian Oxford Dictionary

Diction

There are two meanings for the word *diction* elucidated in the *Canadian Oxford Dictionary*. The first meaning, "the manner of enunciation in speaking or singing," is illustrated by Henry Higgins in the movie *My Fair Lady* when he laments "why can't the English teach their children how to speak?" We, however, are concerned with the second meaning, "the choice of words or phrases in speech or writing."

Consider the following quotation attributed to Johann Wolfgang von Goethe:

"If you wish to know the mind of a man, listen to his words."

Would you agree? If Goethe's statement is true, then surely we ought to be very careful in our choice of words. In communication, our meaning is conveyed in numerous ways, including syntax (the structure of language), word choice, gesture, and tone. It is easy to be hasty in choosing words—to say or write the first thing that pops into your head. George Orwell insists that: "[w]hat is above all needed is to let the meaning choose the word, and not the other way about. In prose, the worst thing one can do with words is surrender to them" (264). In other words, *choose* the words that best express your meaning—don't simply surrender to approximations. I add only this caveat: the first order of the creative process is to get down your ideas, unobstructed by your inner critic. Precision and concision in writing are achieved mainly through the revision process. This is why revision is so necessary. But you will accelerate this process if you attempt to be reasonably precise in your early drafts as long as it does not obstruct the flow of your thoughts.

When looking for a word, instead of going straight to a thesaurus, decide on a word that would be most precise, and then check its meaning in a dictionary. If you know there is a more precise word, but you can't think of it, *then* you can consult a thesaurus. If you go looking with a word in mind, you won't be tempted by a pretentious word. For your writing to sound natural, you must work within your own vocabulary. And remember, you enlarge your vocabulary by reading.

In his well-read and still-relevant article "Politics and the English Language," George Orwell states that what was wrong with the "slovenly language" particular to political writing of his time was "a staleness of imagery and a lack of precision." In his "catalogue of swindles and perversions," he includes dying metaphors—which "save the trouble of picking out appropriate verbs and nouns," pretentious diction, jargon, and meaningless words. In conclusion, he devises four rules that cover most cases. It would be wise to tack these on the wall beside your computer:

1. Never use a metaphor, simile, or other figure of speech which you are used to seeing in print.
2. Never use a long word where a short one will do.
3. If it is possible to cut a word out, always cut it out.
4. Never use the passive where you can use the active voice.

The poet Ezra Pound offers the following advice:

"Fundamental accuracy of statement is the ONE sole morality of writing." ("Past History" 249)

"Good writers are those who keep the language efficient. That is to say, keep it accurate, keep it clear." (*ABC of Reading* 32)

"Incompetence will show in the use of too many words." (*ABC of Reading* 63)

The Virtues of Diction

The Canadian Oxford Guide to Writing

How do we avoid the errors of diction? Thomas Kane, in the *Canadian Oxford Guide to Writing*, states that "when one sins, one sins against the cardinal virtues of diction: precision, of course, but also simplicity, brevity, emphasis, originality, variety" (461).

Here is a quick summary of Kane's rules for avoiding errors in diction:

1. *Make your words as concrete and specific as possible*—not *bird*, but *cardinal*; not *book*, but *Canadian Oxford Dictionary*.
2. *Avoid ambiguity* by avoiding words with two different meanings, general abstractions, pronouns that could refer to two or more antecedents, and structures that induce ambiguity, such as dangling modifiers.
3. *Avoid jargon, barbarism, and clichés*—words and phrases that are obscure, non-existent, used ungrammatically, or overused expressions.
4. *Delete all unnecessary or redundant words* including overlong connectives; unnecessary definitions; vague, general terms; obvious implications (ideas that are clearly implied); wordy modifications; scaffolding (words that explain your intentions, if they are obvious);

introductions to new, unnecessary or undeveloped topics; and strings of unnecessary verbs or verbals.

5. *If you use an idiom, be sure it is used correctly.* Idioms are difficult for foreign-language speakers because an idiom involves one or more words that are used in a sense different from the usual meaning. Native English speakers also err, particularly with prepositions or verbs (for example, not *Eliot gives the image*, but *Eliot creates the image*; in formal writing, not *she says*, but *she states*).

6. *Avoid pretension.* You might think that fancy words will dress up your thoughts, or that convoluted structures will make your writing sound sophisticated, but the opposite it true. Good writing is accurate, clear, and concise.

7. *Avoid awkward-sounding words.* Nothing might be wrong with their meaning, but these words could inadvertently create an awkward sound or rhythm, or an unfortunate rhyme with surrounding words. If it sounds awkward to you, it will sound awkward to your reader.

8. *Be concise.* For example, use a single adjective or adverb instead of a wordy phrase (*he acted unnaturally* instead of *he acted in an unnatural way*); avoid awkward anticipatory constructions (*this is the kind of . . .*); use a single participle instead of a wordy phrase (*it leaves us thinking* instead of *it leaves us with the thought*); do not clutter your main elements with wordiness (*the war caused many changes* instead of *the fact of the war had the effect of causing many changes*).

Discussion Question

Errors in diction are important to avoid. However, even after one has learned to avoid errors, one needs to continue to hone precision and concision. Try this exercise and then discuss the challenges the writing demands: write your life history in 100 words or less.

Exercises

1. Take a page of one of your essays and reduce it by half of its length without losing any meaning. Focus on improving the precision and concision of your writing.

2. Examine an essay that you have written recently. Identify any errors of diction, and correct them. Next, exchange essays with another student and try to find the kinds of errors listed above.

Review

"James Joyce is indeed a black Irishman, wreaking a vengeance, even wilder than the IRA's, on the English language from within, invading the territory of its sanitary ego-presumptions with a flood of impure, dark languages flowing from the damned up sources of collective speech, savagely drowning the ego of the traditional speaker and depositing the property of words in everybody, in the total human community of those who speak and have spoken and shall speak." (Carlos Fuentes)

- In the above quotation, highlight the subject in red and the predicate (finite verb – sentence completion) in blue.
- Circle the finite verb. Is it intransitive, transitive, or linking?
- Identify the verbals.
- Identify the clause(s). Draw a box around the main clause.
- Add brackets around the phrases. What kind of phrases are there and what are they modifying?
- Identify the kind of sentence. Defend your choice.
- Read the quotation aloud and note Fuentes's rhythm—which features create it?
- Explain the use of punctuation. Where does it differ from convention?
- Does Fuentes use any patterns of repetition or other emphatic devices?
- There are two embedded metaphors. The first half of the sentence uses a metaphor of invasion, while the second half employs a metaphor of a flood. Underline the metaphorical language.
- How would you describe the two tenors and vehicles? What is being compared?

Although there are two metaphors in the sentence, this is not an example of "mixing metaphors." It would be a mixed metaphor only if Fuentes had used both invasion and flooding in the first instance, for the first tenor. Notice how he keeps the tenors and their vehicles separate and consistent.

Part Two

Excerpts

Writing is an art and a craft. No matter how skilled you become, divine dissatisfaction never allows you to rest on your laurels; art perpetually strives for perfection. Think of writing as a journey you are on; a path we are all taking. Some are farther down the path than you—these are your best teachers. Good writers are found in every century, every country, and in diverse fields of interest. Good writing is not just found in the classics or academic writing, although these are rich sources. Some of my favourite writers are naturalists like Harry Thurston, scientists like David Suzuki, travel writers like Lawrence Durrell, historical novelists like Dorothy Dunnett, and fantasy writers like J.R.R. Tolkien. To be a good writer you must be an avid reader. When asked for writing advice, the well-known Canadian writer Pierre Berton advised:

"Read! Read! Read! Write! Write! Write!"

However, Ezra Pound maintained that we write what we read. If this is true, then what we read matters. Surfing the Net, reading comics, magazines, and (most) popular fiction may be pleasant escapes, but they will not teach you how to write.

In the next section we will examine longer excerpts as we not only continue to examine grammar's intricacies, but also begin to get a sense of style. There are many definitions of style, and different usages. Here, style is understood as the sum of choices made by a writer; that is, "the way of presenting a subject . . . motivated by the character of the subject, the purpose of the presentation, the reader's qualifications and the writer's personality" (Enkvist et al. 23). As Kane points out, style "is not a superficial fanciness brushed on like a coat of gilt over the basic ideas. Rather than the surface appearance of a piece of writing, style is its deep essence" (*Canadian Oxford Guide to Writing* 11).

There are as many styles as there are writers. But there are two general types that, for our purposes, are useful to compare: the lush, metaphor-rich style of a Dickens or a Clarke and the transparent style of a McKay or a Gowdy. Each writer makes the type his or her own, but they share many qualities. In the first style, the reader notices and delights in the language play, the poetic devices of alliteration and accumulation, the well-crafted figures of speech, the rhetorical and emphatic devices; in the second style, the reader is unimpeded by the writing, as if looking through clear mountain water to the rock bottom. Both types are pleasing to the reader, and require skill to achieve.

I urge you to read and reread the following passages, preferably out loud, until you can hear the rhythm, the cadence, the art of good writing.

26 Don McKay
Clarity

To my mind, there is nothing more important to good writing than clarity. Ezra Pound said, "Good writers are those who keep the language efficient. That is to say, keep it accurate, keep it clear" (*ABC of Reading* 32).

In his remarkable essay "Baler Twine" (from *Vis à Vis*) McKay redefines our concept of wilderness as "not just a set of endangered spaces, but the capacity of all things to elude the mind's appropriation." He moves away from our traditional conceptions in order to refigure our understanding of wilderness, home, and the nature poet. The excerpt that we will examine, which I have drawn out of its much fuller context, is devoted to an example of ravens. First McKay describes his initial encounter with the raven—wild, free, in its natural habitat, a bird that mates for life and calls others to a found carcass, a bird that "arrives like a brash postcard from the wilderness," a talker, folk philosopher, and trickster full of play:

> The first time I saw ravens up close was in Alberta near Blue Ridge, where ten or twelve ravens were playing loop-the-loop. There is a high gravel bank on one side of the river, which must have caused quite a wind bounce, because the ravens were soaring at high speed right at the bank, then, just before impact, shooting up into the air thirty feet or so. They would bail out in that characteristic tumble, clownish, deliberate boys on a raft loss of control, flapping and falling to spill the wind, and fly back across the river to do it all again: the aerial equivalent to an otter slide.

Then McKay describes another encounter:

> Then, on my way back home, I got my best look at a raven. It was hung up by the roadside at the entrance to a lane, a piece of baler twine around one leg, wings spread. There was a huge shotgun hole in its back just above the tail, which was missing altogether.
>
> What do you think I should make of this? It won't do to be sentimental here. But this doesn't fall into an ethic of hunting; nor can it be understood from the rational-cum-aesthetic perspective of someone like Audubon who would shoot individuals of a species in order to have tractable models. Even without the myths which attend this creature, even discounting "the sacred" and setting aside the ancient mariner, this seems very bad. Shooting the raven was one thing: we all know, each of us, that sinister delight in casual brutality and long-distance death. Displaying it was another—controlling its death as well as

Don McKay (b. 1942)

Don McKay is a Canadian poet, professor, editor, and publisher. His many accolades include the Governor General's Literary Award (which he was awarded twice), the Griffin Poetry Prize, and the Order of Canada. An avid birdwatcher and hiker, McKay has been described as an "eco-poet." Poets have long been profoundly connected to nature; however, an eco-poet has a more critical edge, a deeper awareness of environmental crisis, and connects ecology, poetics, and the art of writing. In the same breath, McKay's poetry respects "otherness." In a line from *Strikeslip* we catch a glimpse of his aim in the writing process, seeing it as: "Some act of pure attention . . . simple, naked, perilously perfect."

Gasperau Press

taking its life. Displaying it declares that the appropriation is total. A dead body seeks to rejoin the elements; this one is required to serve as a sign, a human category—a sign which simply says "we can do this." The raven's being, in Martin Heidegger's terms, was not just used, but used up.

So I cut it down. Its wings were large and eloquent, and not like anything I could think of, certainly not like blown-away umbrellas. The feathers, including the lavish neck-flounce, were still very glossy and fine. Its eyes were sphincters of nothing.

Timothy Findley once said that before there can be change, first we have to imagine it. After a rigorous and informed argument, McKay concludes:

Meanwhile I am still standing by the roadside dangling a dead raven, wondering what to do

. . . . There is no ritual imaginable which would, right now, set in balance our relation to Pacific atolls blown up in hydrogen bomb tests, or to clear-cut forests, or to the ecosphere itself. Just find a hollow for the raven where no one is likely to find it; cover it with brush so that it may decompose in private; drive away; think; read. There is imaginative work to be done.

Discussion

What I want to point out in the passages is the lack of sentimentality in the writing, the *clarity*. The language is remarkably efficient. It is clear and accurate. There is no emotive language, no rhetoric, no pathos, and yet, as a reader, I am profoundly moved. McKay describes precisely and concisely (as Einstein said, "make everything as simple as possible, but not one bit simpler"); he lets the images speak for themselves, then moves on to his meditative thoughts.

What keeps it clear and accurate? First, remember Orwell's dictum: never use a long word where a short one will do. You can see in McKay's text that this style prevents the reader from tripping up over words. Not only a pretentious word, but also an inappropriate word, an awkward phrase, or an imprecise choice trips the reader, stalling the flow of ideas. The reader stops, whether consciously or subconsciously, to reconsider the word or to figure out the structure. In all writing, the writer asks the reader to suspend disbelief, to enter their creation, their invention. It is like being suspended in a cloud of words—a precarious relationship—one false move by the writer and the reader plummets out of the created world. And then the writer has to begin all over again the work of rebuilding that relationship, pulling the reader back in and up. Readers will not sanction this disillusionment more than once or twice, and even then it shakes their confidence in the writer.

Second, effective word choice keeps the language clear and accurate. Precise word choice is rarely noticeable to the reader; rather, it is experienced subconsciously in the enjoyment of the reading. The only word that stands out is *sphincters*—partly because it is not a word in most of our vocabularies, partly because it is a little awkward to pronounce at first (sfĭ´ngk´tərs). Like McKay's use of *requited*, we do not trip over the word because it is a precise choice. It is also an interesting choice, full of suggestion. Think of words as magnets that draw others to them. What words does *sphincter* attract? For me, it draws *sphinx* and *sinister*.

The writing probably did not stand out for you the first time, as it does in say Dickens or Dillard, but read the passages again to note McKay's precise choice of verbs, adjectives, and descriptive phrases, his lack of clichés. There is nothing lazy, no approximations, in this writing. This precision also keeps the writing clear and accurate.

There is only one section in this excerpt that we really notice for its literary devices: "They would bail out in that characteristic tumble, clownish, deliberate boys on a raft loss of control, flapping and falling to spill the wind, and fly back across the river to do it all again: the aerial equivalent to an otter slide." Or, more precisely: "that characteristic tumble, clownish, deliberate boys on a raft loss of control, flapping and falling to spill the wind to fly." You know why this is emphatic—the accumulation of adjectives, the paired adjectives, the alliteration, and the figure of speech (*deliberate boys on a raft loss of control*). Again, this is the line the author wants you to remember when you are comparing it to the flagrantly exposed dead raven—those two later unadorned sentences, objective in tone, cutting swiftly and accurately to the heart.

You will likely notice other devices subtly at work in the passages. McKay refers to two well-known figures—the wildlife artist John James Audubon and the philosopher Martin Heidegger—and alludes to the poem "The Rime of the Ancient Mariner" by Samuel Taylor Coleridge. One sentence stands out as being the most densely packed, in terms of allusion: "Even without the myths which attend this creature, even discounting 'the sacred' and setting aside the ancient mariner, this seems very bad." You do not have to know these allusions to get the gist, but it deepens the meaning immeasurably if you recognize them. For example, "The Rime of the Ancient Mariner" is one of the great English poems that heralds modern poetry and English Romanticism; it is a tale of fantastic events experienced by a mariner on a sea voyage. It begins with a grizzled old sailor stopping one of three wedding guests and forcing him to listen to a strange tale from his past. In his story, the ancient mariner is aboard a ship that is driven south, off course, by a storm and enters a "rime"—a strange, icy patch of ocean in Antarctica. A large white bird with a great wingspan—an albatross—appears, to lead them out of the polar region. One day, on impulse, the mariner shoots the bird. The needless death arouses the wrath of spirits who send the ship into uncharted waters, where it is becalmed. The crew, desperately thirsty and blaming the mariner, force him to wear the dead albatross around his neck. After a time, the ship encounters a ghostly vessel carrying Death and the "Nightmare Life-in-Death," who are playing dice for the souls of the crew. Death wins all except the mariner—he must endure a life-in-death as punishment for killing the albatross. The crew members die, but the mariner lives on, seeing the curse in the dead eyes of his fellow shipmates. Finally, after the mariner sees sea snakes swimming in the water and blesses them, showing his respect for the natural world, the albatross falls from his neck. The bodies of the crew, possessed by good spirits, rise and steer the ship home, but on sight of land the ship sinks in a whirlpool, leaving only the mariner behind. He is rescued, but as penance for shooting the albatross, the mariner is forced to wander the earth and recount his story.

You can see how this brief mention of "the ancient mariner" enriches McKay's meaning enormously, yet efficiently. Once you know the story, two words bring all of its events and meaning to mind and to bear on the text.

McKay suggests many other tales in his reference to "myths which attend this creature" and "the sacred." The raven belongs to many cultures—Greek, Egyptian, Norse, Celtic, Japanese, Inuit, and Haida, to mention a few. It has a long history. It is a warrior bird in *Beowulf*; it is sent out by Noah during the flood and much earlier by Gilgamesh; it is a messenger to Apollo, once white but turned black by the god's misplaced anger; the ravens Hugin (thought) and Muin (memory) sit on the shoulders of Odin in Norse mythology; and, of course, the raven is the trickster—creator and destroyer—in many North American First Nations' mythologies. Even setting all this aside, states McKay, the death still "seems very bad." Indeed.

McKay's argument is persuasive because it is measured, objective in tone, honest in its descriptions, and effective in its examples and allusions. The writing does not get in the way. We see clearly through it, as through mountain water, to the solid rock bottom of his argument.

27 Charles Dickens
Emphatic Devices

We only have to look at the opening pages of Charles Dickens's most famous story, *A Christmas Carol*, to discover his mastery of emphatic devices.

Stave 1: **Marley's Ghost**

Marley was dead: to begin with. There is no doubt whatever about that. The register of his burial was signed by the clergyman, the clerk, the undertaker, and the chief mourner. Scrooge signed it. And Scrooge's name was good upon 'Change for anything he chose to put his hand to.

Old Marley was as dead as a door-nail.

Mind! I don't mean to say that I know, of my own knowledge, what there is particularly dead about a door-nail. I might have been inclined, myself, to regard a coffin-nail as the deadest piece of ironmongery in the trade. But the wisdom of our ancestors is in the simile; and my unhallowed hands shall not disturb it. or the Country's done for. You will therefore permit me to repeat, emphatically, that Marley was as dead as a door-nail.

Scrooge knew he was dead? Of course he did. How could it be otherwise? Scrooge and he were partners for I don't know how many years. Scrooge was his sole executor, his sole administrator, his sole assign, his sole residuary legatee, his sole friend, and sole mourner. And even Scrooge was not so dreadfully cut up by the sad event, but that he was an excellent man of business on the very day of the funeral, and solemnised it with an undoubted bargain.

The mention of Marley's funeral brings me back to the point I started from. There is no doubt that Marley was dead. This must be distinctly understood, or nothing wonderful can come of the story I am going to relate. If we were not perfectly convinced that Hamlet's Father died before the play began, there would be nothing more remarkable in his taking a stroll at night, in an easterly wind, upon his own ramparts, than there would be in any other middle-aged gentleman rashly turning out after dark in a breezy spot—say Saint Paul's Churchyard for instance—literally to astonish his son's weak mind.

Scrooge never painted out Old Marley's name. There it stood, years afterwards, above the warehouse door: Scrooge and Marley. The firm was known as Scrooge and Marley. Sometimes people new to the business called Scrooge Scrooge, and sometimes Marley, but he answered to both names: it was all the same to him.

Charles Dickens (1812–1870)

© *The Print Collector / Alamy*

Charles Dickens is regarded as the English language's most celebrated novelist. His life is well-known, from his appalling experience at 12 years old in a boot blacking factory, after his father was sent to debtor's prison, to his affair with the actress Ellen Ternan, and separation from his wife, Catherine Hogarth. He worked as a journalist and editor as well as a writer, and owned a theatrical company that featured the performance of *The Frozen Deep* for Queen Victoria. He was a supporter of social reform, especially for desolate women and children's rights. But he is best known for his stories of the downtrodden, struggling in nineteenth-century London. Dickens' themes draw readers to the oppression of the poor, betrayal, prejudice, and to dismal and dangerous working conditions; he challenged authorities to address the living conditions of the marginalized in Victorian England. Near the end of his life he embarked on a number of demanding reading tours that, because of failing health, hastened his death.

Oh! But he was a tight-fisted hand at the grind-stone, Scrooge! a squeezing, wrenching, grasping, scraping, clutching, covetous, old sinner! Hard and sharp as flint, from which no steel had ever struck out generous fire; secret, and self-contained, and solitary as an oyster. The cold within him froze his old features, nipped his pointed nose, shrivelled his cheek, stiffened his gait; made his eyes red, his thin lips blue and spoke out shrewdly in his grating voice. A frosty rime was on his head, and on his eyebrows, and his wiry chin. He carried his own low temperature always about with him; he iced his office in the dogdays; and didn't thaw it one degree at Christmas.

External heat and cold had little influence on Scrooge. No warmth could warm, no wintry weather chill him. No wind that blew was bitterer than he, no falling snow was more intent upon its purpose, no pelting rain less open to entreaty. Foul weather didn't know where to have him. The heaviest rain, and snow, and hail, and sleet, could boast of the advantage over him in only one respect. They often "came down" handsomely, and Scrooge never did.

Nobody ever stopped him in the street to say, with gladsome looks, "My dear Scrooge, how are you? When will you come to see me?" No beggars implored him to bestow a trifle, no children asked him what it was o'clock, no man or woman ever once in all his life inquired the way to such and such a place, of Scrooge. Even the blind men's dogs appeared to know him; and when they saw him coming on, would tug their owners into doorways and up courts; and then would wag their tails as though they said, "No eye at all is better than an evil eye, dark master!"

But what did Scrooge care! It was the very thing he liked. To edge his way along the crowded paths of life, warning all human sympathy to keep its distance, was what the knowing ones call "nuts" to Scrooge.

Once upon a time . . .

Discussion

It takes Dickens a page and a half to actually begin his story—what Clarke Blaise calls the "then," the "cracking of the perfect, smug egg of possibility" (26)—*Once upon a time . . . .* What has he done in that page and a half? Well, in the first four paragraphs he has told us, explicitly, four times that Marley is dead. Who gets away with that kind of emphasis now? And yet, each time, more information is revealed and we are inexorably drawn into the ghost story. Dickens then uses an allusion to one of Shakespeare's plays—the reference to Hamlet's dead father appearing on the ramparts to Hamlet—to foreshadow Marley's appearance to Scrooge. The next paragraph subtly shifts our focus from Marley to Scrooge. The following paragraphs are a brilliant, flamboyant description of one of literature's best-loved characters. Why? What is it about Scrooge of which we never tire? Yes, of course, his transformation, his reclamation, like the prodigal son, back into the folds of love and compassion. But for us to feel the full impact of this transformation, we must be very clear about what Scrooge is in the beginning: "a squeezing, wrenching, grasping, scraping, clutching, covetous, old sinner!"

I wonder how many times Dickens read those lines out loud to get them right. What **emphatic devices** are at work? Accumulation, certainly, but Dickens also uses paired adjectives (*hard* and *sharp*), alliteration (*wintry weather*), simile (*solitary as an oyster*), and rhythm.

Who can forget the lines Dickens uses to introduce his most famous character: "Oh! But he was a tight-fisted hand at the grind-stone, Scrooge! a squeezing, wrenching, grasping, scraping, clutching, covetous, old sinner! Hard and sharp as flint, from which no steel had ever struck out generous fire; secret, and self-contained, and solitary as an oyster." Look at the effect of isolation in his placement of *Scrooge!* in the middle of that sentence. He uses three exclamation marks—one for the beginning interjection, one in the middle of the sentence, and one at the end. And yet, do we find the mechanical emphasis overused? No, because this is precisely what he needs his readers to remember. For what is revealed in the story is that Scrooge is not just a cold villain; rather, he has redeeming, passionate emotions, repressed for decades. His transformation happens only after he allows his loneliness to emerge and his remorse to begin.

How else does Dickens accomplish his purpose in the opening passage? Look at the way he uses form to enhance his meaning through emphasis and cadence, drawing in the reader, focusing attention. The first sentence contains both an inversion (*Marley was dead: to begin with*) and an announcement (the use of the colon). Hard to ignore that first sentence! The passage also contains a figure of speech (*dead as a door-nail*); although a cliché—a comparison so overused we no longer make the comparison—Dickens forces us to make the comparison by wittily over-examining the phrase in the next sentence. He further uses an allusion, which is also an analogy—the ghost of Hamlet's father precipitates the action, as catalyst, in the play, in the same way that Marley's ghost precipitates the action that transforms Scrooge.

We find patterns of repetition (*no wind . . . no falling snow . . . no pelting rain; no beggars . . . no children . . . no man or woman; his sole executor, his sole administrator*); parallel constructions (*froze his old features, nipped his pointed nose, shrivelled his cheek, stiffened his gait*); and patterns of threes (*A frosty rime was on his head, and on his eyebrows, and his wiry chin. He carried his own low temperature always about with him; he iced his office in the dogdays; and didn't thaw it one degree at Christmas*).

However, it is not only emphatic devices that shape Dickens's style. Note his variety in sentence kinds, styles, and lengths. One of Dickens's many skills is his flawless ability to use a variety of sentence kinds and sentence lengths within a paragraph, and then to vary the kind and length of the paragraphs. In that variation, he captures the speaking voice without ever losing the richness of the more complex written word. This, perhaps, is the device that most distinctly creates his style.

I could write an entire book on grammar using only examples from this opening passage, but suffice it to say: if you want to learn what language can do, read Dickens.

After reading Dickens's excerpt, you might think "that's all well and good, but Dickens is a storyteller. I'm writing essays, and, furthermore, this is not the 1800s." But the fact of the matter is that the devices have been around for a very long time, and good writers, in every century and discipline, make them their own.

In this lesson, we will examine an excerpt from Peter Sanger's essay, "A Knowledge of Evening," which appears in his work of nonfiction, *White Salt Mountain: Words in Time*. The excerpt embodies Ezra Pound's dictum: "keep it accurate, keep it clear," as well as Gustave Flaubert's dictum: "whatever you want to say, there is only one word to express it," which makes Sanger's writing a joy to read for its diction alone.

Like Dickens, Sanger begins with a short simple sentence to gain our attention. Here, too, is the piece of information we need to keep in mind: *The eagle tree is down*. The opening description prepares the reader for an analogy that Sanger draws later in his essay, where words are compared to eyries. However, we will examine just the opening description of two eagles, a pine tree, an eyrie, and a hurricane:

> The eagle tree is down. A hurricane broke it in September. Three-quarters of its one-hundred-and-fifty-foot height was shorn away. Only a stalagmite spar tipped by a yellow shard of heartwood is left upright.
>
> The eagle tree was a white pine. It grew from the side of a cliff of red mud and sandstone on the southern side of Cameron Creek at a point two wing-beats away from the creek's outflow into the tidal flux of the Shubenacadie River. Where the pine's uttermost canopy grew most strongly and closely, the eagles had built an eyrie. It was an involute bravura of sticks, tree limbs, brush-wood, driftwood, and feathers. In size, by distant appearance, it looked like a beaver lodge grappled out of a pond and dumped upside down to wedge by weight in the pine's cross-trees.
>
> I had watched the eyrie for fifteen years, beginning on a December day just after my wife and I and son had moved onto a small farm located ten min-utes walk away to the north. I visited the eyrie almost every day afterwards, observing it from a cliffed plateau which overlooks Cameron Creek intervale. Hidden, sometimes, among the spruce, young maples and stunted cicatriced

Peter Sanger (b. 1943)

Peter Sanger is a Canadian writer, professor, historian, editor, and critic. He has an impressive corpus, including seven books of poetry, non-fiction work, critical texts on Robert Outram, and edited works on Elizabeth Bishop and John Thompson. He has been poetry editor for *The Antigonish Review* since 1985. He is Professor Emeritus at the Nova Scotia Agricultural College where he taught for 30 years.

Gaspereau Press

In a review in *Quill and Quire*, Zachariah Wells describes Sanger's language in *Aiken Drum* and *Earth Moth* as filled with "taut structures, lyric compression, complex syntax, perspicuous diction, and an instinct for the marriage of sound and sense possessed only by genuine poets." For Wells, Sanger is "one of the country's most underappreciated talents." Dalhousie University bestowed an Honourary Doctorate to Sanger in 2012, with these words, "Peter's life and work encourages us to seek that beautiful balance between living and thinking, to engage the world around us and to express what we see with wit and clarity."

beech, I watched the pair of eagles rebuild the eyrie in March. I watched them share incubation. I watched one or the other sitting on the eggs in late March and April when quick squalls would cover the sitting bird's back and shoulders with snow and his or hunting mate would fly in suddenly low through thick, wet flakes carrying a shad or eel in its talons as if the world was entering an iced apocalypse. I watched the pair feeding, beak to beak, each of their two young with precise patience and gentle proffer a parent must learn to teach a child how to eat with a fork. And sometimes I saw the yellow, depthless iris of an eagle's eye through my telescope and knew that I was being watched, as something central to sight, but peripheral to meaning.

As something incomplete. I should have known better.

Discussion

Like Dickens, Sanger uses a variety of sentence kinds and lengths, along with figures of speech, rhythm, analogy, allusion, anaphora, and other emphatic devices. However, his style is very distinct from that of Dickens. It has the clarity and accuracy of a scientist, the literary finesse of a poet, and the intellectual depth of a scholar—an intoxicating combination.

Sanger begins with a number of short sentences, drawing us in. The concrete, vivid, personal example of the eagle tree hooks us before we encounter the later, more abstract, argument. After describing the eagle tree, Sanger uses that enticing "*I should have known better*" to move on to his main argument, in which the eagle tree is used as an analogy. As the essay progresses, the writing becomes increasingly abstract, but at the point where he might lose some of his readers, Sanger returns to his concrete beginning. In scholarly writing, this balance is particularly crucial—a delicate dance between the concrete and the abstract. You should think about that balance in your own writing—where would a concrete image or example be useful?

When you want to keep your writing accurate and clear, your choice of **diction**, your word choice, becomes paramount. But this is also a balance. Orwell said to always use the shorter word, but that does not necessarily mean using the simpler word. We are not after a "dumbing down." You should take accuracy and precision as your guides.

Sanger is precise in both his realistic and his imaginative details. The scientific exactness with which Sanger describes the tree's location is followed by a more literary interpretation, where distance is measured in "wingbeats." And doesn't the switch from the literal to the figurative feel natural? It is Sanger's precise choice of words, his accuracy in diction, that keeps you, the reader, engaged.

Also note that Sanger never resorts to approximations: for example, "Hidden, sometimes, among the spruce, young maples and stunted cicatriced beech, I watched the pair of eagles rebuild the eyrie in March." He could have easily left out *sometimes*, but that would have reduced the writing to an approximation—he couldn't watch at all times, he wouldn't always be hidden, and he probably didn't always watch from the same spot. The interruption also slows the reader's pace, throwing emphasis back on *hidden*, and acting almost like a colon announcing the anaphora.

Sanger reminds us of words we might have forgotten or have become too lazy to use, lovely, precise words like *shorn* and *bravura* and *grappled*. He also introduces us to new words like *cicatriced*, meaning, in this context, marks left by the healing of injured tissue; *intervale*, meaning a low-lying tract of land along a river; *proffer*, as a noun, meaning an offer; and *involute*, meaning complex and intricate but also curved inward or spirally—a precise choice to describe a nest. This is the kind of writing that increases your vocabulary.

Of course, Sanger's writing reveals many other elements and devices. Let's look briefly at three: anaphora, unconventional use of commas, and choice of title.

The third paragraph is an excellent example of a modern-day use of anaphora—repeating a clause (*I watched*) at the beginning of successive sentences. "I watched" signals not only what the narrator saw, but also the passage of time. The paragraph pleases rhythmically, not only in the structure of the anaphora, but also in the break caused by the short, abrupt sentence—"I watched them share incubation"—in the midst of longer, flowing sentences.

Next, consider how Sanger uses **commas**. In writing, there are some punctuation conventions one ought not to break, such as using a period at the end of an indicative sentence or a question mark at the end of an interrogative, or omitting commas when using a restrictive phrase. But modern usage allows greater choice in other instances. The comma, already acknowledged as the most complex punctuation mark, is also the most flexible—making it all the more confusing. Conventionally, the rules are straightforward, and if you follow them, no one will complain.

However, good writers make stylistic choices that don't always conform to the rules. Sanger, for example, depends less on conventional rules and more on a combination of breath, effect, and meaning to guide his use of the comma. We learned that a comma should be used to set off non-restrictive phrases and clauses, but look at this sentence:

> I watched one or the other sitting on the eggs in late March and April when quick squalls would cover the sitting bird's back and shoulders with snow and his or hunting mate would fly in suddenly low through thick, wet flakes carrying a shad or eel in its talons as if the world was entering an iced apocalypse.

Conventionally, if we marked every phrase and clause, it would look like this:

> I watched one or the other, sitting on the eggs, in late March and April, when quick squalls would cover the sitting bird's back and shoulders with snow, and his or hunting mate would fly in suddenly low, through thick, wet flakes, carrying a shad or eel, in its talons, as if the world was entering an iced apocalypse.

If you read this new construct out loud, you will notice that the use of so many commas completely changes the rhythm—the flow becomes choppy, the reader is slowed down, and the emphasis shifts to elements that Sanger does not want to emphasize. The structure of the anaphora is such that Sanger wants his reader to see and understand this particular unit as just one in a list of similar units, weighted the same, as in a compound structure. He doesn't want his reader to slow down at this point.

To use commas creatively, your best guide is your breath. Ask yourself, what effect do I want, where do I want the emphasis to fall, and how does the choice affect meaning? You need to know the rule or convention that you are breaking, and why you are breaking it—it must be a *choice* to use or not use a comma, not an accident. Most importantly, the choice to delete a comma should not make the meaning muddier for your reader.

Finally, consider Sanger's evocative *title*. "A Knowledge of Evening" is a significant and multi-layered element, an allusion drawn from St. Augustine's *The City of God*, used and explained later in Sanger's text. Your best choice for a title is a crucial concept, a figure of speech, or another significant element drawn from the heart of your text. This is why you should title your essay after it is completed. If you feel that you need a title to focus your writing at the beginning, create a working title, and then refine it in revision.

29 Harry Thurston
Description

In his remarkable book, *Tidal Life: A Natural History of the Bay of Fundy*, Harry Thurston examines the natural and human history of a threatened ecosystem, teaching newcomers and life-long residents alike to see and appreciate—and hopefully protect—the beauty of the Bay of Fundy.

The following passage opens Thurston's chapter on the fragility of habitat. In it, he describes the massive flocks of sandpipers that come to select spots on the Fundy Shore to feed and get fat for a few weeks in late July before their long migration south. Thousands of "peeps" congregate in a single flock, making the beach "a living pulse" and the sky "a storm of wings" when the birds rise in flight. Thurston's description of the sandpipers is a superb example of how description can be used effectively not just in literature, but in many kinds of writing:

An aerial dance, a grand ballet of flight performed by tens of thousands of mercurial dancers, storms my vision: the peeps have returned to Fundy. They are a flock of semipalmated sandpipers, a dark cloud of wing beats that creates its own musical wind. Their speed is startling, and the swift beating of their two-toned wings, flickering first white, then dark, produces a stroboscopic effect as unsettling as the rapid eye movement of a dream. The mist of birds grows denser, darker, then thins out like a summer storm cloud buffeted and frayed by high winds. The flock has an infinite elasticity that allows it to charge shape constantly as well as a magnetic cohesion that draws it back to an ever-changing centre. The eye delights at the constant metamorphosis. Flying low over the water, the flock abruptly spirals upward like a tornado; at the zenith of its curving climb, it seems to explode in all directions like a flowering of fireworks; then, pulled together by an inseparable bond, the birds continue their peregrination of the Bay in long wavy banners of flight.

Flying wing to wing, each bird seems miraculously to anticipate its neighbours next move so that none seems to lead and none to follow. Executing this impossibly intricate choreography, the flock becomes one body, supremely alive and in touch with all its parts.

Suddenly—and with uncanny precision—the sandpipers bank, revealing their white underbellies; instantly the dark cloud becomes a silver cloud. In the strong light the effect is of thousands of palm-sized mirrors turned to the sun in unison, then turned again to show their dark sides. It is a constantly changing light show, engineered to take advantage of every caprice of breeze.

Harry Thurston (b. 1950)
Harry Thurston is a Canadian writer, poet, and free-lance journalist. He has taught poetry at St. Mary's University and Journalism at University of King's College, Halifax and was writer-in-residence at Acadia University, Mount Allison University and the Haig-Brown writer-in-residence in Campbell River, BC. He is internationally renowned for his nature writing and his feature articles in leading journals, including *Audubon* and *National Geographic*. His many awards include the Canadian Science Writers' Association's Science in Society Award, the National Magazine Award for Science and Technology, the Evelyn Richardson Prize for non-fiction (awarded four times), the Sigurd Olson Nature Writing Award, and the Gulf of Maine Council on the Marine Environment, Visionary Award, "for increasing public awareness on environmental issues." In 2013, Acadia University bestowed on him a Doctor of Literature for outstanding contributions to his community and beyond. George Elliott Clarke, reviewing *If Men Lived on Earth* (2000), has this to say about Thurston's language, "The lines are clear, thought-through, elemental, irrefutable. They transform history, economics, and ecology into experienced truth . . . ."

Image by Michael Fuller

Discussion

The *Canadian Oxford Guide to Writing* notes a number of elements to practise for writing effective description: "selecting significant, concrete, vivid details that appeal to the senses; using precise diction; naming specifics; and then organizing these details using a guiding principle" (Kane 154). Reread the excerpt, and take note of how effectively Thurston uses these devices in his writing.

Description is often delineated into *objective* (with the emphasis on the subject itself) or *subjective* (with the emphasis on the writer's response). We might at first want to label Thurston's description as subjective—after all, he writes in the first person and we expect to witness a personal investigation. However, I think this would be faulty. Although the writing is not what we often associate with objective—that is, formal or removed—it *is* focused on the subject. It is impersonal in the sense that, despite Thurston's obvious delight and awe, the description itself is not about his response. Don't mistake me—subjective description is not inferior; it can have great power. Edward Abbey, for instance, in *Desert Solitaire*, recounts what he did in Havasu Canyon, a branch of the Grand Canyon, for five weeks, alone, in subjective description every bit as powerful as Thurston's objective description. It just has a different role.

Regardless, all description requires a *logical progression*—preferably one that follows the organization inherent in the subject itself. Perhaps the most important element in description is the organization—where to start, proceed, and end—and its guiding principle: why. Good description begins with a broad look at the subject. The next step depends on the nature of the subject. Some subjects are straightforward; they have an obvious structure to follow—for example, when describing a tree you could begin with the largest element, the trunk, then proceed to the ever-smaller parts: limbs, twigs, leaves, and buds. You can also use this straightforward structure in your essays; for example, to describe a theory you could start with the most important principle and proceed to the lesser principles—or vice versa.

Thurston begins the description with an overview of the most noticeable trait, the amazing shift of dark to light as the peeps bank in flight to reveal their light underside. He has chosen a very difficult subject because it is constantly changing—shape, colour, even direction. But look at how well we follow his eye, even if we have never seen sandpipers, particularly after he describes both the infinite elasticity and magnetic cohesion that allows the flock in flight to change on a whim yet stay as one body, one "banner of flight." This is his guiding principle. Organizationally, the point of view remains constant as we watch, from an advantageous distance, the unfolding of the flock's "light show."

We can examine Thurston's writing to learn other elements that are also crucial to effective description.

First, notice how Thurston's writing appeals to the *senses*, inviting the reader to share in his experience, effortlessly. Reread the excerpt and identify the two senses that Thurston arouses. Note the variety of visual sensations (many of them metaphors): the dance, the ballet, the dark cloud, the summer storm cloud buffeted and frayed, the tornado, the fireworks, the banner of flight, the mirrors, the light show. Note also the impact of the auditory detail: the sound of the swift beating of wings. Why do you think that Thurston chooses not to appeal to any of our other senses here?

Next, examine the *precision* in Thurston's writing. We might think that nature writing depends even more than other writing on naming specifics; certainly, we can see here the necessity of being precise—*mercurial dancers*, *semipalmated sandpipers*, *the swift beating of the two-toned wings*. However, this precision is significant in many forms of writing. All argument, for example, is strengthened by specifics, accuracy, and precise word choice.

Thurston, like Sanger, is also precise in his choice of *diction*. Read the passage again. Which words are particularly effective? Why? What parts of speech are they? Note that no word in Thurston's description, even if unknown to us, seems forced or pompous (*semipalmated, stroboscopic, peregrination*); this is because each word is the precise choice. Reading good writing, seeing these words used effectively in context, is one way our vocabulary grows naturally.

Note also how Thurston used figurative language to enhance his description by making the reader see certain details in a different way. None of Thurston's figures of speech are clichés; they are unexpected but appropriate, creating delight while enhancing our understanding.

Finally, consider Thurston's choice of **tense**. His use of the *present tense* is immediate and intimate—we feel like we are there, watching with him. This feeling is enhanced by the first-person point of view. This narrative perspective—first-person present tense—combined with Thurston's vivid, sensual details and his accurate and precise diction create a highly realistic, personal experience for the reader.

30 Doris Lessing
Flow

Every year, CBC Radio invites one writer, usually one engaged in political and social change, to give a series of lectures as part of the Massey Lectures series. Since its creation in 1961, the series has featured both Canadian writers, such as Charles Taylor, Margaret Atwood, Thomas King, and John Ralston Saul, and sterling international writers, such as Carlos Fuentes, Claude Lévi-Strauss, R.D. Laing, Martin Luther King Jr, and Doris Lessing.

Lessing's Massey Lecture, "Prisons We Choose to Live Inside," is a persuasive argument for personal freedom and individual action in a world where stepping outside one's community beliefs leads to ostracism or worse. The prisons "we choose to live inside," Lessing argues, are those seemingly "impregnable systems of thought," the status quo, our community's binding beliefs. In a world saturated with advertising designed to manipulate every "choice" we make—from the clothes we wear to the politicians we vote for—Lessing urges her listeners and readers to consider stepping outside and resisting, despite the risk, in order to critically assess mass slogans, mass ideas, mass movements, the mob mentality of blindly following the leader.

The excerpt we will examine is taken from Lessing's conclusion, but I urge you to read the whole lecture, and, indeed, to read others in the Massey series. They are excellent examples, composed by great writers, of how to use effective form to enhance your meaning:

> It is particularly hard for young people, faced with what seems like impervious walls of obstacles, to have belief in their ability to change things, to keep their personal and individual viewpoints intact. I remember very clearly how it seemed to me in my late teens and early twenties, seeing only what seemed to be impregnable systems of thought, of belief—governments that seemed unshakeable. But what has happened to those governments—like the white government in Southern Rhodesia, for instance? To those powerful systems of faith, like the Nazis, or the Italian Fascists, or Stalinism? To the British Empire—to all the European empires, in fact, so recently powerful? They have all gone, and in such a short time.
>
> Looking back, I no longer see these enormous blocs, nations, movements, systems, faiths, religions, but only individuals, people who when I was young I might have valued, but not with much belief in the possibility of their changing

Doris Lessing (1919–2013)

One of Britain's most complex, diverse, and prolific writers, Doris Lessing published a wide and compelling range of writing, including short stories, novels, plays, poems, essays, translations, librettos, and television scripts. Born in Persia to British parents, she was raised in Zimbabwe, dropping out of boarding school at 13 to work as a nanny, telephonist, office worker and journalist, while she established herself as a writer. Remarkably, she became a self-educated intellectual of very high regard. Also an anti-nuclear campaigner, her anti-apartheid activism led to her being banned from South Africa and Southern Rhodesia (1956–1993). A political writer, her novels explore race conflict, nuclear arms, and gender. Her novels are diverse in form and genre, employing realism, the psychological thriller, science fiction and what she called "inner-space fiction." Her many awards include France's Prix Médicis étranger, Spain's Prince of Asturias Prize in Literature, the Nobel Prize for Literature (2007), and the British Order of the Companions of Honour.

© *Interfoto/Alamy*

anything. Looking back, I see what a great influence an individual may have, even an apparently obscure person, living a small, quiet life. It is individuals who change societies, give birth to ideas, who, standing out against tides of opinion, change them. This is as true in open societies as it is in oppressive societies, but of course the casualty rate in the closed societies is higher. Everything that has ever happened to me has taught me to value the individual, the person who cultivates and preserves her or his own ways of thinking, who stands out against group thinking, group pressures, or who, conforming no more than is necessary to group pressures, quietly preserves individual thinking and development.

I am not at all talking about eccentrics, about whom such a fuss is made in Britain. I do think that only a very rigid and conforming society could have produced the idea of an eccentric in the first place. Eccentrics tend to be in love with the image of eccentricity, and once embarked on this path, become more and more picturesque, developing eccentricity for its own sake. No, I am talking about people who think about what is going on in the world, who try to assimilate information about our history, about how we behave and function— people who advance humanity as a whole.

It is my belief that an intelligent and forward-looking society would do everything possible to produce such individuals, instead of, as happens very often, suppressing them. But if governments, if cultures, don't encourage their production, then individuals and groups can and should . . . . Such people, such individuals, will be a most productive yeast and ferment, and lucky the society who has plenty of them.

Discussion

Notice the flow of Lessing's work, how smoothly the text moves from paragraph to paragraph. There are two main elements of good flow: 1) compatible ideas that flow logically and 2) unified paragraphs. Understanding and
utilizing these two basic principles will increase the flow of your own writing
immeasurably.

In Lessing's conclusion, each paragraph flows logically from the previous
one; there is a logical progression of ideas. The first paragraph discusses the
difficulties of changing one's perspective, the second describes the type of person who can make changes, the third defines who Lessing does and does not
mean, and the final paragraph concludes with her main point—the benefit of
a society consisting of thinking individuals. This logical flow is supported by
Lessing's use of transitional sentences at the beginning and end of her paragraphs. It is not necessary to have a transitional sentence in every paragraph,
but a few select placements can help guide the reader through the argument.

Lessing also constructs each paragraph as a unified, complete thought. In
your own writing, practise paragraph unity by constructing each paragraph
so it has a topic sentence that introduces the main idea of the paragraph; fill
out the paragraph by developing this idea with explanation, examples, and
illustrations; and use a transitional sentence where necessary to set up the
next paragraph.

There are a number of other devices that contribute to Lessing's distinct
style.

First, let's examine how she used different forms of **repetition**. At the
beginning of this conclusion, it is crucial that Lessing undermines our belief in
the impregnable systems of thought that imprison us; hence, the repetition of
seemed four times in the first two sentences. Does the repetition work for you?
What was your reaction before the repetition was pointed out? Do you think
the repetition worked subliminally to prepare you for Lessing's final conclusion? Writers must edit out this kind of repetition if it is done unwittingly,
as it makes the writing monotonous and flat; but used with a purpose, it can
be effective.

Lessing also uses **anaphora** in her repetition of "Looking back." The first
"Looking back" highlights her authority based on experience, but this sentence
ends in an aside. The repetition refocuses our attention on Lessing's main idea.

The **rhythm** of the piece is set by a rhythm of twos. Throughout, Lessing
enhances this rhythm by repeating *structures* of two—paired adjectives (*intelligent and forward-looking*; *rigid and conforming*; *small, quiet*) and paired
nouns (*individuals and groups, yeast and ferment*).

Lessing's repetition of *who* clauses creates pleasing rhythms, but this also
reinforces the meaning. The *who* clauses, considered together, efficiently define

and summarize what she means by *"an individual"*—the *"who"*—engaged in individual action.

> "It is individuals <u>who</u> change societies, give birth to ideas, <u>who</u>, standing out against tides of opinion, change them."

> "Everything that has ever happened to me has taught me to value the individual, the person <u>who</u> cultivates and preserves her or his own ways of thinking, <u>who</u> stands out against group thinking, group pressures, or <u>who</u>, conforming no more than is necessary to group pressures, quietly preserves individual thinking and development."

> "No, I am talking about people <u>who</u> think about what is going on in the world, <u>who</u> try to assimilate information about our history, about how we behave and function—people <u>who</u> advance humanity as a whole."

Turn your attention to the *individual sentences* in the passage. Note how Lessing varies sentence length within the paragraph to create variety and flow. Her emphatic sentences—a short simple sentence, a periodic sentence, a question, an interruption, a fragment—are all used sparingly.

Next, consider Lessing's *point of view*. The subject matter—personal freedom and individual action—almost demands to be examined in the first person. Lessing's use of the first person point of view is also immediate and personal, without becoming unduly subjective. This point of view is a style choice Lessing has made to bridge the gap between herself and her listener and reader.

Finally, remember that this excerpt was intended as the conclusion to an *oral presentation*. You read Lessing's passage, but think how it would sound over the radio. What adjustments do you think a writer should make for an oral presentation? Note the carefully selected use of fragments, informal diction (*fuss*), and contractions (*don't*). All are used effectively to lighten the oral presentation, but sparingly so as not to lose the voice of authority or the more complex patterns of the written word.

31 Barack Obama
Parallel Constructions, Anaphora

One of United States' President Barack Obama's many talents is pitching his speech at the right level for his audience. But regardless of whether he is speaking to the houses of Congress or to schoolchildren, he uses the rhythm of parallel constructions and anaphora to not only provide clarity and emphasis, but also create the rhythm that helps give his speech its emotive quality—its impact. Notice his use of these devices in the following speech, broadcast on television to school children across the United States on 8 September 2009:

Now, I've given a lot of speeches about education. And I've talked a lot about responsibility. I've talked about your teachers' responsibility for inspiring you, and pushing you to learn. I've talked about your parents' responsibility for making sure you stay on track, and get your homework done, and don't spend every waking hour in front of the TV or with that Xbox. I've talked a lot about your government's responsibility for setting high standards, supporting teachers and principals, and turning around schools that aren't working, where students aren't getting the opportunities they deserve. But at the end of the day, we can have the most dedicated teachers, the most supportive parents, and the best schools in the world—and none of it will matter unless all of you fulfill your responsibilities. Unless you show up to those schools; pay attention to those teachers; listen to your parents, grandparents, and other adults; and put in the hard work it takes to succeed.

And that's what I want to focus on today: the responsibility each of you has for your education. I want to start with the responsibility you have to yourself. Every single one of you has something you're good at. Every single one of you has something to offer. And you have a responsibility to yourself to discover what that is. That's the opportunity an education can provide. Maybe you could be a good writer—maybe even good enough to write a book or articles in a newspaper—but you might not know it until you write a paper for your English class. Maybe you could be an innovator or an inventor—maybe even good enough to come up with the next iPhone or a new medicine or vaccine—but you might not know it until you do a project for your science class. Maybe you could be a mayor or a senator or a Supreme Court justice, but you might not know that until you join student government or the debate team. And no matter what you want to do with your life—I guarantee that you'll need an education to do it. You want to be a doctor, or a teacher, or a police officer? You want to be a nurse or

Barack Obama (b. 1961)

Barack Obama was elected the 44th president of the United States in 2008, re-elected to a second term in 2012, serving as the first African American to hold American Presidential office. Born in Honolulu, Obama graduated from Columbia University, majoring in international studies, and Harvard Law School. He was a community organizer in Chicago and a civil rights attorney before becoming a state senator for Illinois, and subsequently served in the American Senate.

© Kristoffer Tripplaar/ Alamy

In his first term as President, Obama faced a national crisis in the form of a major recession and responded with legislation including economic stimulus, job creation, and tax relief. He initiated health-care reform, ended military involvement in the Iraq War, and ordered the military operation which killed Osama bin Laden. He won the Nobel Peace Prize in 2009.

As Obama attests, language matters. His keynote address at the Democratic Convention in 2004, for instance, won him national attention and a stellar rise to the presidency.

an architect, a lawyer or a member of our military? You're going to need a good education for every single one of those careers. You can't drop out of school and just drop into a good job. You've got to work for it and train for it and learn for it.

And this isn't just important for your own life and your own future. What you make of your education will decide nothing less than the future of this country. What you're learning in school today will determine whether we as a nation can meet our greatest challenges in the future.

Discussion

There are two key constructions that you should note in Obama's speech: parallel construction and anaphora.

First, consider the **parallel constructions**—where Obama repeats exact grammatical patterns. They provide clarity, create pleasing rhythms, and contribute to the emotional impact of the piece. In writing, as in speeches, this is one of your most useful constructs. You can parallel words, phrases, clauses, or whole sentences.

A parallel construction not only has the same grammatical form, but also the same grammatical relationship; that is, the parallel constructs play the same role in the sentence. In his speech to schoolchildren, Obama parallels primarily verbals and verb phrases, such as "*inspiring you*"/"*pushing you*" or "to *work for it* and *train for it* and *learn for it*." Note that the repeating construction does not have to contain the exact same words—only the exact grammatical structure: "*show up to those schools, pay attention to those teachers, listen to your parents.*" Parallel constructions organize thoughts economically and clearly, *if* the ideas themselves are logically parallel.

However, it is not always possible to retain the parallel construction throughout—meaning or rhythm might require a slight adjustment. When this is the case, a writer will use what is called a *balanced construction*—not exact parallelism, but constructs that are similar in form, relationship, and length. For example, the following sentence (a fragment that completes the previous sentence) begins with a *parallel construction*, but ends in a balanced construction: "*Unless you show up to those schools; pay attention to those teachers; listen to your parents, grandparents and other adults*; and put in the hard work it takes to succeed."

When you are acquiring the skill of parallel constructions, keep your parallels exact. English speakers prefer rhythm created by constructs of two or three elements. As you begin to deliberately use parallel constructions in your writing, try to create patterns of two or three words, phrases, or clauses.

Now consider Obama's use of **anaphora**. In the short excerpt quoted above, Obama uses anaphora four times: "*I've talked a lot about (responsibility) . . .*"; "*every single one of you . . .*"; "*Maybe you could be . . .*"; "*You want to be . . .*". This, of course, would be too many for a written work, but is effective in speech. Written text benefits from these constructs, but they must be used sparingly and with more finesse and subtlety.

An anaphora is noticeable—use it to introduce shifts in argument, to emphasize, or to highlight. For example, in a speech to the American public in January 2009, Obama begins by stating:

> Throughout America's history, there have been some years that simply rolled into the next without much notice or fanfare. Then there are the years that come along once in a generation—the kind that mark a clean break from a troubled past, and set a new course for our nation.
> This is one of those years.

Next, he outlines what is wrong in the country, and then he shifts to how he will improve the situation. He introduces this major shift to the positive with an anaphora—"*That is why*"—which he pulls throughout the entire second half of the speech:

> That is why we need to act boldly and act now to reverse these cycles. That's why we need to put money in the pockets of the American people, create new jobs, and invest in our future. That's why we need to re-start the flow of credit and restore the rules of the road that will ensure a crisis like this never happens again.

Notice how not only the anaphora but also the parallel constructions aid rhythm and clarity; notice also that Obama uses patterns of twos and threes.

32 Annie Dillard
Poetic Devices in Prose

The Writing Life is Annie Dillard's semi-autobiographical description of the writing process—exquisitely crafted anecdotes brilliantly illuminating the writer's tasks. Here is a virtuoso we can admire and learn from. Note her use of rhythm, internal rhyme, repetition, and figurative language in the following excerpt:

> Who will teach me to write? a reader wanted to know.
>
> The page, the page, that eternal blankness, the blankness of eternity which you cover slowly, affirming time's scrawl as a right and your daring as necessity; the page, which you cover woodenly, ruining it, but asserting your freedom and power to act, acknowledging that you ruin everything you touch but touching it nevertheless, because acting is better than being here in mere opacity; the page which you cover slowly with the crabbed thread of your gut; the page in the purity of its possibilities; the page of your death, against which you pit such flawed excellences as you can muster with all your life's strength; that page will teach you to write.

Discussion

There are many devices that we think of as belonging to poetry that good prose writers utilize to give their text richness, excitement, and flair. The three we have focused on in this text are rhythm, repetition, and figurative language. Let's take one last look at these devices.

If Dillard were a musician, we would say she has perfect pitch. Read the above quotation out loud a couple of times to hear what I mean. Her skill is in knowing how to effectively use not only sound devices such as assonance (rhyming vowel sounds, for example the long *a*) and alliteration (*the page in the purity of its possibilities*), but also **rhythm** and **cadence**. Rhythm consists of light and heavy stresses—remember that heavy stresses should fall on content-rich words. Cadence is the tonal inflection, the rise and fall of the phrase. This excerpt could be a prose poem. (By the way—reading poetry, and poetic prose, will help you improve your writing's rhythm. Reading your writing aloud will also help.)

Dillard also varies her sentence or clause lengths to create a pleasing rhythm and cadence—but she does not use random variation—they are chosen to enhance her meaning. In this excerpt, for example, generally, the

Annie Dillard (b. 1945)

Annie Dillard is an American novelist, poet, and, most notably, nonfiction writer. In 1975, at 29, she won the Pulitzer Prize for General Nonfiction for *Pilgrim at Tinker Creek*, a nonfiction narrative about the natural world near her home in Roanoke, Virginia. This modern classic is a good place to start one's reading of Dillard, an exceptional, incantatory author whose books have been translated into more than ten languages. Timothy Findley described her as "an oracle who rightly confounds as much as she comforts, using her questions and observations to urge us on toward our own answers about the world we live in—and about why and how we might better understand our place in it."

Richard Howard/Time & Life Pictures/Getty Images

clauses grow shorter, picking up speed as they move toward the paragraph's climax. Variation is crucial. In your own writing, check each paragraph to see if you are varying not only sentence length, but also sentence openings. This is a common problem for novice writers. If too many sentences begin with the same grammatical pattern (say, subject/verb: *He states, Cohen believes, He is*), you can create monotony—unless, you are deliberately using repetition to create a monotonous effect.

Take a closer look at Dillard's use of **repetition**. Note how she repeats "the page"—notice how these words sound in the paragraph, and how, by varying the length of her clauses, Dillard keeps the words from becoming uncomfortably repetitious. Rather, as the clauses pile up, the repetition helps give shape and emphasis to her conclusion. Both the accumulative form and the rhythm aid in throwing the emphasis on "*that* page" and then these devices fall gracefully to suggest "here comes the denouement." Dillard also uses anaphora to help create a pleasing and effective cadence. The anaphora "*which you cover*" is used three times: "*which you cover* slowly," "*which you cover* woodenly," and "*which you cover* slowly." The variation in the participial phrases and clauses that complete each thought prevents this anaphora from becoming monotonous.

Let's pause for a moment to review patterns of **repetition**. Good writers do not write well by chance. Like any good craftsperson or artist, they use the tools they have been bequeathed, working daily, honing, waiting for the moment of inspiration when all their practice will come to fruition and the tool will be used effortlessly in the service of meaning.

The patterns of repetition first came down to us via the ancient Greeks, particularly through Aristotle's *Rhetoric* and *Poetics*. But these devices are not antiquities to be condescendingly nodded to and ignored. Nor is rhetoric something to be scoffed at; although the word is often used loosely and negatively, the wise writer knows rhetoric's place. Today, we tend to think of *rhetoric* as *rhetorical fallacy* (or errors), rather than a valuable skill. The *Canadian Oxford Dictionary* acknowledges this current negative connotation—it first defines rhetoric as "the art of effective or persuasive speaking or writing," then adds, in a second entry, "often with an implication of insincerity or exaggeration." On the contrary, rhetoric devoid of its fallacies is a powerful tool in the pursuit and expression of truth. One of its devices is repetition.

Repetition plays an intricate and complex role in writing, and a good place to start your study is with the patterns of repetition. We can divide these patterns into two main types: those that express the same idea in different words, and those that express an idea using the same repeated word, of which there are many forms. Dillard, like Dickens, is a master of these forms. Consider the beginning of Dillard's second sentence: "The page, the page, that eternal blankness, the blankness of eternity . . . ." In this example alone there are three patterns of repetition at work:

- **diacope**, where the same term is separated by one or two other words (*blankness, the blankness*);
- **polyptoton**, where a word is repeated in a different form (*eternal* [adjective]/*eternity* [noun]); and
- **epizeuxis**, where the same term is repeated immediately (*the page, the page*).

Finally, let's consider effective use of **figurative language**. Dillard never resorts to clichés. One source of her consummate skill is her powerful use of metaphorical language, her ability to create the perfect vehicle for her tenor: "the page which you cover slowly with the crabbed thread of your gut."

One technique to rid your writing of clichés and other tired expressions is to surf your writing specifically looking for these phrases, highlight them, and then go back and rethink them when you have time. Creating metaphorical language at first seems a formidable task, but it is learned through practice. It is not something you do heedlessly or inattentively, at least, not before you have deliberately stowed away observations, facts, and trivia to be retrieved later. I like to collect these details from well-researched television programs, such as those on Oasis and National Geographic Television; magazines such as *The Walrus*; the Harper's Index online; photography; and books of facts. But they are everywhere—those lovely vehicles just waiting for you to hook them up with the perfect tenor.

Let me give you an example. I was looking at an incredible photograph of an immense, threatening black cloud over the prairies that turned out to be a flock of birds—which, apparently, began from one pair of starlings brought over from Britain—and my first thought was: what would it be like for an imported bird released into the wild—do their instincts fail them? I wrote it down in my journal, knowing it was a possible vehicle. Then I waited for the tenor. It came a little later, when I noticed my aging father confused over a simple task. The simile became: As we age, the simple things elude us, like imported birds whose instincts fail them. One day, I will adapt this simile and use it in a poem or a work of prose.

33 Phil Fontaine
Eloquence, Tense

The following speech, which Phil Fontaine delivered in 2008 to the House of Commons in response to the government apology for the suffering inflicted by the enforced residential schools, demonstrates Fontaine's powerful, eloquent mastery of oration. His response is full of dignity, honesty, and courageous hope, a hope that has persevered with the First Nations since the arrival of the Europeans, and the desecration of the Aboriginal way of life:

> Prime Minister, Chief Justice, members of the House, elders, survivors, Canadians: for our parents, our grandparents, great grandparents, indeed for all of the generations which have preceded us, this day testifies to nothing less than the achievement of the impossible.
>
> This morning our elders held a condolence ceremony for those who never heard an apology, never received compensation, yet courageously fought assimilation so that we could witness this day. Together we remember and honour them, for it was they who suffered the most as they witnessed generation after generation of their children taken from their families' love and guidance. For the generations that will follow us, we bear witness today in this House that our survival as First Nations peoples in this land is affirmed forever. Therefore, the significance of this day is not just about what has been but, equally important, what is to come. Never again will this House consider us the Indian problem just for being who we are.
>
> We heard the government of Canada take full responsibility for this dreadful chapter in our shared history. We heard the prime minister declare that this will never happen again. Finally, we heard Canada say it is sorry. Brave survivors, through the telling of their painful stories, have stripped white supremacy of its authority and legitimacy. The irresistibility of speaking truth to power is real. Today is not the result of a political game. Instead, it is something that shows the righteousness and importance of our struggle. We know we have many difficult issues to handle. There are many fights still to be fought. What happened today signifies a new dawn in the relationship between us and the rest of Canada. We are and always have been an indispensable part of the Canadian identity. Our peoples, our history and our present being are the essence of Canada. The attempts to erase our identities hurt us deeply, but it also hurt all Canadians and impoverished the character of this nation.

Phil Fontaine (b. 1944)

Phil Fontaine, past national chief of the Assembly of First Nations, is a highly respected Canadian political leader. He has been honoured with many awards, holding five honorary doctorates and membership in the Order of Manitoba. During his remarkable political career, Phil Fontaine helped establish the first Aboriginal-controlled education system in Canada, a locally controlled child and family services agency, and the first on-reserve alcohol and addictions treatment centre. He negotiated the first comprehensive self-government plan for Manitoba First Nations and signed historic employment equity agreements, which resulted in thousands of job opportunities for First Nations citizens. He negotiated a fair and just process for the settlement of specific land claims and brought together First Nations from across the continent to sign the Declaration of Kinship and Cooperation among the Indigenous Peoples and Nations of North America. Most recently he negotiated a successful resolution and settlement of claims arising out of the 150-year Aboriginal residential school tragedy.

© Design Pics Inc./Alamy

We must not falter in our duty now. Emboldened by this spectacle of history, it is possible to end our racial nightmare together. The memories of residential schools sometimes cut like merciless knives at our souls. This day will help us to put that pain behind us. But it signifies something even more important: a respectful and, therefore, liberating relationship between us and the rest of Canada. Together we can achieve the greatness our country deserves. The apology today is founded upon, more than anything else, the recognition that we all own our own lives and destinies, the only true foundation for a society where peoples can flourish. We must now capture a new spirit and vision to meet the challenges of the future. As a great statesman once said, we are all part of one "garment of destiny." The differences between us are not blood or colour and "the ties that bind us are deeper than those that separate us." The "common road of hope" will bring us to reconciliation more than any words, laws, or legal claims ever could. We still have to struggle, but now we are in this together.

I reach out to all Canadians today in this spirit of reconciliation.

Meegwetch.

Discussion

To understand Fontaine's skilled oration, let's begin by examining *modes of expression*. There are three traditional modes of expression, or rhetorical styles, that the writer can draw upon to enhance meaning: satire, pathos, and eloquence. Satire evokes feelings of contempt and disdain in order to ridicule and censure the follies and vices of society. Pathos evokes feelings of pity, tenderness, or sorrow. Eloquence evokes our noblest sentiments. In modern times, these modes are most commonly found in speech writing.

Fontaine's speech is primarily written in the rhetorical style known as eloquence (also used in Martin Luther King Jr's famous "I have a dream" speech). Fontaine's words appeal to our ideals and noblest sentiments. However, they also evoke pathos—feelings of pity and sorrow.

Some of the syntactic devices Fontaine employs to accomplish this complex tone are the devices of repetition, such as anaphora (*we heard*); parallel constructions; and patterns of twos—particularly nouns (*love and guidance, generation after generation, spirit and vision, blood or colour*)—which help create the rhythm.

I will leave you to consider Fontaine's use of **tense** on your own, based on what we have discussed in previous lessons, but I would like to present an additional example for your consideration. Recently, I came across a remarkable little chapbook published in 2008, entitled *I Got It from an Elder: Conversations in Healing Language.* The back cover describes this work as a "poetically shaped collage of conversations about the healing tense in the Mi'kmaq language, and an attempt to integrate indigenous and Western ways of knowing." After months of wrestling with English grammar, I was struck by this incredible tense, this "healing tense" that has no equal in the English language. This is the way Murdena Marshall explains it:

> See, in the Mi'kmaq world, in all Native worlds, you have to give recognition to everything: misdeeds, good deeds, past deeds you know? Anything. You have to give that acknowledgement. Everything that you do, you have to acknowledge. Because you have the opportunity to be in any of these tenses. (Iwama et al. section 9)

A Mi'kmaq speaker, she explains, will understand which state of reality a fellow Mi'kmaq speaker is in depending on his or her use of tense.

She gives an example, admitting that she is using "the worst verb in the non-Native world, when you talk about Indians"—to be drunk. "This is how they see us all the time, being drunk. So I took that being drunk and called it *ketkiya*, which means *I am drunk*" (Iwama et al. section 18). She supposes the example of Johnny, who is drunk, but when confronted by his mother, denies it, leaves, and doesn't return until four days later. When he does return, things change, but not until he takes full responsibility for his actions. His family ostracizes him until he acknowledges his behaviour with the use of the healing tense. When he says *ketkiyayasnek* ("I was really drunk, Mom") he uses a tense that acknowledges his error:

When he goes into this tense, then my attitude has to change. Because he has taken his misdeeds and placed them in front of him. And then he walks around them. Then he tells me, yes, I was there . . . . Everybody in the household, everybody in the room has to abide with him. Because it is a very vulnerable position to be in this. His spirit becomes like jello, like jelly. You throw a drop of hot water and it will dissolve. And he could very well get up again and go get stinkin' drunk and come back and say, look everybody, this is what you all predicted. (Iwama et al. section 19)

. . .

And so you try to protect his spirit from injury of any kind. And he could be in this tense for half a day, for the rest of the evening. As long as it's that –nek, when the tense is –nek, your attitude has to change, to soothe his spirit and reinforce his spirit, that he is forgiven and loved. (Iwama et al. section 21)

English could use a tense like *nek*. A tense through which—if I had the courage to use it, and by so doing acknowledge my actions, show my remorse, try to become better—my spirit would be immediately soothed. I would be supported by those around me, my family and friends morally bound to the act of forgiveness. And ultimately—through remorse and forgiveness that these acts of the heart express in the *nek* tense—I would know that I am forgiven and loved. The use of the *nek* tense requires a deep-rooted honesty and trust.

34 Thomas Carlyle
Last Word

Writing is a complex art. It is also holistic. One must continue to develop all its elements simultaneously. There is only one way to develop any art or craft and that is to practise.

It is the capacity to persevere that reaps the greatest rewards. When Carlyle completed his famous three volume historical work, *The French Revolution*, the text that propelled him into fame, he gave the manuscript to a friend, the philosopher John Stuart Mill, to read. This was in 1834 when there was no duplicate, no backup copy. Somehow, the manuscript was taken for waste paper and burned. Did Carlyle despair? No, he sat down and wrote it all, by hand, draft after draft, again.

As in any art, you must believe in yourself. You are unique; and you have something to say. In *Sartor Resartus* Carlyle gives good advice that still holds true today:

> Produce! Produce! Were it but the pitifullest infinitesimal fraction of a product, produce it, in God's name! 'Tis the utmost thou hast in thee: out with it then. Up, up! Whatsoever thy hand findeth to do, do it with thy whole might. Work while it is called Today; for the Night cometh, wherein no man can work.

Culminating Activities

1. Rewrite Carlyle's quotation using current language, but retain the urgency, repetition, and rhythm of his distinct style. Compare your results with those of your classmates and discuss how you made your choices.

2. What is style but the sum of a writer's choices? Who do you think of, when asked to name a writer with a distinct style? Perhaps you recall a writer from your childhood—A.A. Milne (*Winnie the Pooh*) or Beatrix Potter (*The Tale of Peter Rabbit*). If you grew up reading strong writers, you can probably still hear their cadence, remember their particular sense of humour, bathe in the old joy of nestling down in bed and sinking into the pleasure of their language—even if you can't remember one line now. A writer's style is unique; a good one stays with us. For example, do you recognize this?

Thomas Carlyle (1795–1881)

Thomas Carlyle, a Scottish man of letters, historian, critic, satirist and sociological writer of the Victorian Age was a Tory, a Calvinist, and a man of many contradictions. Carlyle was educated at the University of Edinburgh, where later he served as Rector. With his wife, Jane Welsh (also a satirist), he lived in London, where he was known as the *Sage of Chelsea*. Their home was a centre for a broad literary circle. Carlyle is best known for his satirical writing and histories.

© *GL Archive/Alamy*

Dickers, it is said, used Carlyle's *The French Revolution* as a primary source for *The Tale of Two Cities*.

In *British Authors of the Nineteenth Century*, Carlyle's style is characterized as, ". . . an extraordinary farrago, leaping not flowing, coining strange words and performing extravagant evolutions; yet cumulatively it impresses as a great style, suffused with humor, irony, and passion; impossible to imitate, utterly personal, burning, and convincing." (Kunitz and Haycroft 118)

"Unless someone like you cares a whole awful lot, nothing is going to get better. It's not."

Even if you haven't read *The Lorax*, if you've read other works by Dr. Seuss, then you cannot mistake the author. Seuss's style resides in his choice of ironic rhyme, his rhythm, his subject, and his humorous stresses (*whole awful lot*). Now think of the academic writers you are reading. Which ones stand out not only as good thinkers—but as good writers? Find an academic writer whose text you enjoy reading, and figure out what makes the writing appeal to you. List five elements, and provide an example for each one.

3. List three elements that you believe are most necessary for good writing. Be prepared to defend your choices in a class discussion. There is no right answer here, just persuasive arguments. As G.K. Chesterton once said about writing, "There is only one thing necessary: everything." Still, if you were going to work on three aspects, which would you deem most necessary? The following is an incomplete list of elements from which you might choose: clarity, variety of sentences, effective diction, rhythm, parallel constructions, concision, precision, powerful figures of speech, effective punctuation, emphatic devices, tone. What other elements might you choose?

Part Three

Essay Writing

The word "essay" originates from the Latin word "exagium," which implies the notion of "weighing." Its modern definition denotes a relatively short prose composition on any subject, expressing fact or opinion. As Edwin Schlossberg put succinctly, "The skill of writing is to create a context in which other people can think." One purpose of the essay is to provide common ground where discussion takes place. Writing an essay is exhilarating—you, the author, set the boundaries and give the best argument, as you believe it to be.

On a more sobering note, the essay is the primary tool for evaluation in many learning institutions. Why is this? The essay allows students to demonstrate not only that they have assimilated class material, but also that they can synthesize the knowledge they have acquired, presenting their thoughts in an analytical, critical form. The essay demonstrates how well you read, listen, think, and write. For this reason alone, it is worth learning how to write an essay well. But learning to write well has other benefits. As E.M. Forester said: *"How do I know what I think until I see what I say?"*

Ten Rules of Thumb for Essay Writing

1. Effective **topics** arise from the course material, your interest and insight.
2. Every good essay has a strong **thesis statement**.
3. Working from an **outline** makes your task easier (and will increase your grade!).
4. An essay's **beginning** should capture your reader's attention and interest.
5. The middle of the essay will **flow** if you stick to your outline and take care to craft your paragraphs.
6. All **quotations** must be integrated within your argument, and cited.
7. A **conclusion** needs to sound like **The End** and must be coherent with your thesis statement.
8. The time to craft your **title** is after you have a complete draft.
9. **Documentation** is central to the integrity of your work.
10. **Revision** is the underrated step that most significantly improves your grade.

Writing an essay initially requires collecting material, thinking about what you want to argue, then outlining, drafting, revising and editing. Let's consider this process in more detail.

1. Finding a topic.

If you have been given a **topic** skip to the next point. Otherwise use the methods of brainstorming and free writing to explore ideas. Ideas may be discovered in your text's table of contents or class discussions. But remember that the best essays have the feel of commitment. Once you have an idea that appeals to you, start by drawing diagrams and clustering to explore associations. Ask questions such as: What is the scope of the topic? What is it like/unlike? What part most intrigues me? What do I already know that I can draw to this topic? Are there examples I can use? What are the implications of various theses? This is the creative stage, so put your inner critic aside and let ideas flow without judgement. Jot down as many ideas as you can before looking for secondary sources. Remember that the best essay advances your ideas, supported by experts. At this stage, too many secondary sources may confuse and overly influence you.

2. Crafting a thesis statement.

The process of finding a topic leads to the writing of a **thesis statement**; a sentence or two that state what you argue in the essay. Ensure that the thesis is narrow enough to be discussed thoroughly in the designated length, but not so narrow that you have very little to say. Avoid banal or uninteresting theses, and over-generalizations. Your thesis statement is a contention, something you want to prove. It is often placed as the last sentence in the introduction, but not always. Insure that it is readily identified and not tangled up in the other introductory comments.

If you are having difficulty focusing and limiting your topic, try this method: 1) decide on a topic; 2) choose one aspect; 3) list three main reasons that you can use to support your thesis. For example:

Topic	one aspect	three main ideas for support
Terrorism	definition of "terrorism"	the nature of acts of violence, theories on point of view, and arguments in favour of your moral stance.

The three main ideas for support will give your essay a three part structure.

How do you turn the topic into a thesis statement, a contention? One method is to pose a question.

Thesis statement: Is the label "terrorism" dependent on one's point of view or do all acts of violence, particularly against citizens, deserve the label terrorism?

This question/statement allows the expression of a *working* thesis. It will need to be refined in the revision process, as our thinking often evolves in writing; however, a working thesis allows you to begin.

3. Writing an outline.

Without an **outline** your essay easily loses shape—the difference between haute couture and sweat pants. Too often an outline is skipped. There are two types of outlines in effective essay writing; scratch and formal. A scratch outline is a simple sketch of what you will do, and in what order. Use it in an examination situation or whenever you need to write quickly. For a formal essay, however, employ a formal outline. It is the blueprint for an essay. It insures coherence, flow, logic, and successful execution.

- A formal outline has a formal structure consisting of headings typically in the following pattern:
  1
     A
        1
           a

- Headings are aligned vertically by equal weight. Each of these headings can be increased:

2
   A
      1
         a
         b
      2
         a
         b
   B etc.

- The first word of each heading has a capital. The heading of a paragraph is a complete sentence.

Once you have established the formal structure, now turn to content. An outline is a guide, not something writ in stone. The adaptation of the formal structure will depend on your purpose. The first thing to note is what kind of an answer is expected: a comparison, interpretation, definition, explanation? Remember, whenever you are given a topic, *to answer the question*. It is a matter of identifying the purpose of the essay. Consider the following topics in a variety of disciplines. Each purpose requires a different approach:

English: **Compare and contrast** the motives of Katniss and Peeta in *The Hunger Games*.

History: **Discuss** the conflicting theories of Joan of Arc's voices and messages.

Politics: **Define** the role of interest groups in democratic politics.

Science: **Identify and discuss** three concepts essential to understanding the Laws of Thermodynamics.

Engineering: **Explain** three unique problems encountered with the building of the Alaska Highway and how they were solved.

Once you have a basic outline you need to flesh it out. Now is the time to turn to experts in the field.

Consider an example of a formal sentence outline in English literature.

The Devil in Timothy Findley's Not Wanted on the Voyage.

Thesis statement

In Timothy Findley's *Not Wanted on the Voyage* one might think that Lucy (Lucifer in drag) represents the Devil. However, Findley reverses such traditional roles to reveal inherent prejudices in patriarchy.

A formal sentence outline might, accordingly, advance the view that:

1. In Book One the reader suspects Lucy is Lucifer.
    A. The first intimation that he/she is Lucifer occurs with her appearance in the wood.
        1) We discover Lucy has webbed fingers and only angels have webbed fingers.
        2) His/her first instinct, we discern, is to kill.
    B. However, Lucy's true nature is revealed when Michael Archangelis appears in the wood, calling Lucy "brother."
    C. By the end of Book One we see Lucy as Lucifer disguised as a seven foot five drag queen ready to marry Ham in order to secure a place on the Ark.

2. Initially, one assumes that Noah is the good guy, the man of God, based on our knowledge of the Biblical story.
    A. We are told that his name is Noah Noyes (read No/Yes).
    B. Noah is chosen by Yaweh, an Old Testament name for God.
    C. Noah undertakes the actions of the Biblical story: building an Ark; getting animals on board two by two; making sacrifices.

3. However, not all is as it seems; even before the Ark sails, there are hints that Noah is not all goodness and light. Once secluded on board the Ark, the characters' personalities become intensified and their true natures emerge.
    A. Lucy becomes a source of comfort and hope on board.
        1) He/she makes friends with all the misfits—the demons and the unicorn.
        2) He/she creates light in the darkness of the hold and resurrects the unicorn.
        3) He/she teaches the others about the need for tolerance.
    B. Noah is more interested in protecting his power than doing the right thing.
        1) He invents orders from Yaweh, and titles for himself.
        2) He prevents the faeries and Mottyl who is blind from entering the Ark.
        3) We learn that he has already disposed of one of his offspring, an ape child, and that he has married Emma to Japeth so he can blame her genes on any deformity should it occur in their offspring.
        4) The reader tends to excuse Noah's early actions as being those of a hard man of God—until he murders Lotte.

4. Findley's provocative retelling of the Noah's ark tale shocks us into re-examining the heart of patriarchy: fear of losing power.
   A. Noah tries to eliminate or control anything that he sees as threatening his power and authority.
   B. By the end of the story, Noah is revealed as a tyrant.
      1) He attacks the dolphins, convincing Shem that they are enemy pirates.
      2) He treats women as objects to serve and obey him: first Mrs. Noyes and then, even more horrendously, Hannah.
      3) He throws Hannah's baby overboard not only because it might reveal his abuse, but more importantly because, if the truth be told, it would reveal a weakness in himself.

Conclusion

We are told in the opening prologue that "Everyone knows it wasn't like that . . . ." Findley's retelling of Noah's Ark is not the biblical story; although, it makes one rethink it.

A. The reversal of Lucifer and Noah turns the traditional story upside down in order to reveal inherent prejudices in patriarchy.
B. At the heart of Findley's critique of patriarchy is man's fear of losing power. Noah reveals what some people are willing to do to maintain power. Here indeed is the devil.

Note: when you write your actual essay, do not use numbers and letters.

This is just an outline. Now each of the claims must be supported and developed.

Notice how, in an interpretative essay, the argument develops as you simultaneously move through the novel or short story. Following the chronology of the text assures that your reader does not get lost, that you do not repeat your examples and illustrations, and the weight of your argument builds with the growing tension, complexity and power of the novel as it builds toward its climax.

4. Beginning.

Endings are elusive, middles are nowhere to be found, but worst of all is to begin, to begin, to begin. (Donald Barthelme, "The Dolt," *The New Yorker*)

"The first paragraph is a microcosm of the whole, but in a way that only the whole can reveal." (Clark Blaise, "To Begin to Begin")

A **good beginning** should clearly identify, given the topic, the context you are entering and what you want to argue within that context. But it does not reveal everything. Scholarly essays should create some tension, inducing the desire to read on. A good beginning includes: 1) an introduction to your topic that captures your reader's interest, 2) your thesis statement, and 3) a plan of execution, implicitly or explicitly stated; that is, the order in which you will develop your thesis. Note that a three part structure for your thesis statement informs the reader of the order of what will be discussed.

In the *Canadian Oxford Guide to Writing*, Thomas Kane suggests ways to arouse scholarly interest:

1. **Stressing the importance of the subject**; as John Peale Bishop does in his essay on Picasso: "There is no painter who has so spontaneously and so profoundly reflected his age as Pablo Picasso."
2. **Arousing curiosity**; for example, by using a cryptic remark that combines clarity of statement with mystery of intent, as in Hilaire Belloc's essay "The Barbarians" which begins, "It is a pity true history is not taught in the schools."
3. **Amusing your reader with a witty remark** often alluding to a historical, literary, or scholarly figure, as does Colin Cherry's beginning of *On Human Communication*: "Leibnitz, it has sometimes been said, was the last man to know everything."

But take care not to be more dramatic than the argument of your essay allows. Consider the following student example: is the opening paragraph an effective beginning? Did the writer present a context to situate the argument, while capturing your interest? What is the thesis statement? Is there a plausible plan of execution?

In Alistair MacLeod's collection of short stories, "The Lost Salt Gift of Blood," MacLeod emphasizes the dichotomy between relic and traditional values of the older generation, with the adventuresome and often idealistic perspectives of the youth. Central to many of MacLeod's short stories are the matriarchs of these families, though often thought of as "supporting actresses" These women want their families to be close, both in spirit and proximity. Ironically, it is this desire for an insular existence that alienates them from their families. The mother in "The Boat" exemplifies this estrangement, which she both causes and endures. The loss of family the mother experiences can be attributed to her uncompromising and close-minded perspectives, overvaluing of trad-itional principles and her sense of duty.

Note here the funnel effect, moving from the broad topic to a specific thesis: MacLeod's collection, matriarchs, mother in "The Boat," thesis.

5. Making the essay flow.

Once you have established your topic, thesis, outline and introduction, much of the hard work is done. Now it is a matter of following your outline and craft-ing paragraphs. What you most need, in the middle of the essay, are coher-ence and flow. Use this rule of thumb: three well developed paragraphs per page. This will insure that your paragraphs are neither too long (shapeless) nor too short (undeveloped). Each paragraph needs a main idea. This does not always have to be the first sentence. This main idea should be the next logical step in your argument. However, simply stating a point is not convincing; you must develop and support it. Develop your paragraph's idea by using explana-tion, description, analysis, qualification or definition; support it with reasons, illustrations, examples or direct quotations by experts. Don't make every para-graph exactly the same—this becomes tedious.

6. Integrating quotations.

Quotations that you use come from the text and secondary sources recognized as authorities on the subject. (In a short English interpretative essay, most quotations will come from the text itself, to support your claims.) Be select-ive; find the most authoritative voice and use the best quotation you can find. Do not take shortcuts. First determine who constitutes an expert. Beware of unscholarly on-line resources. Use books, articles in periodicals and scholarly journals, either from the library shelves or online. Just make sure the source is an expert. Any quotation you choose should speak directly to your point, sup-porting it, adding something significant to give your argument weight.

In an English literature essay, quotations also give the reader a taste of the writing itself; therefore, do not use just short phrases or single sentences. Periodically, use a longer quotation (four to six lines) that also reveals the writer's style.

Integrate quotations smoothly into the essay. Think of an integrated quota-tion as having three parts: introduction, middle, comment. The middle is the quotation, itself.

Consider finding the three parts in the following example:

Timothy Findlay's provocative story about Noah's ark begins with a disclaimer: "Everyone knows it wasn't like that. To begin with, they make it sound as if there wasn't any argument; as if there wasn't any panic—no one being pushed aside—no one being trampled—none of the animals howling—none of the people screaming blue murder" (Findlay 3). Findlay immediately engages his reader by raising questions: who is "everyone"; who are "they"? How do we know it wasn't like that? Is this what we are about to encounter—panic, howl-ing, people screaming blue murder?

A quotation ought not to stand alone; it must be bracketed by introduction and comment. The longer the quotation, the more developed the introduction and comment should be. Even with a short one, there must be an effective weaving of the quotation into your sentence structure. Briefly introduce what you want your reader to note or who is speaking, and after you quote it, make a comment about its relationship, significance, or textual power. Make sure your reader knows why you are using this particular quotation; it is obvious to you, but not self-evident to others. Don't make your reader do the work for you. Example:

> Hannah does what she is told, believing that this is the way that she might share in patriarchal power. The price she pays, however, is to become party to Noah's reign of terror on board. The death of Lotte serves as a good example: "It was Japeth who killed her. And although Mrs. Noyes would never forgive her—Hannah hadn't been party to what happened, she had merely done what she was told and carried Lotte through the portal, wrapped in the blanket" (Findley 168). Hannah, we know, didn't actually use the knife that slit Lotte's throat, but she was still partly to blame. Her mistake was in thinking that she could partake in power, if only she kept her head down, did as she was told and didn't ask questions. Even before Noah abuses her, however, her gain in status is minimal: it can not compensate for her loss of companionship and respect, or her feeling of self-loathing.

A few more pointers:
1. Quote exactly. This is an area for zero tolerance for error.
2. Use the words of critics and experts to support *your* ideas, not the other way around.
3. Use quotations sparingly. Don't use two or three in a row; one suffices, if well chosen. Use no more than one long or two short quotations per paragraph, and not every paragraph should have one. Vary the type of support; for example, employ paraphrase as well as direct quotations.
4. Punctuation and layout for quotations must follow your documenting style: see your chosen style guide.
5. Take special care to cite your paraphrase or the quotation's source to avoid the charge of plagiarism.

7. Ending.

A short essay requires a brief conclusion; longer dissertations require more summation. It is imperative that your ending be coherent with your thesis statement. To make your conclusion *sound* like an ending:

a) **Use signal words** at the beginning of your final paragraph, such as *In conclusion, Finally.*

b) **Return to your thesis**, summing up your argument concisely; re-state the implications, consequences or inferences briefly, focusing on your strongest arguments. In a longer essay, you may relate them to the broader context of your topic.

c) **Use rhythmic variation**; for example, if the final paragraph consists of longer, complex sentences, end with a short emphatic one. Or end a long summing up sentence with a spondee (three stressed syllables) at the very end to give it the weight of an ending.

8. Inventing an effective title.

A good title achieves two purposes: it 1) clearly identifies the main idea of the essay and 2) arouses reader interest. The title for an English literature essay should include the text and author you are analysing or interpreting. It should point to the main idea in your essay. Try to be specific: what is the essence of your argument? Consider as an example: "Survival versus compassion in *The Hunger Games* by Suzanne Collins." Note title, author and main idea; but, does it capture your interest?

9. Citing and documenting.

Most of what you need to know about **documentation** can be found online or in the library. However, it is important to know that documenting requires a recognized style. Commonly employed styles include the Modern Language Association (MLA), University of Chicago, and American Psychological Association (APA). However, disciplines tend to have a preferred style, so check with your instructor. Each style has its own guidelines, which include the layout of the essay (margins, spacing, indentation), how to cite sources throughout the essay, and how to document your sources (books, articles from journals, lines of poetry, online articles) in a bibliography.

Be exact with documentation. This is another area of zero tolerance for error. Formats are available; follow them exactly, and be consistent. The use of one style approved by your instructor provides consistency, causes as little distraction from the writing as possible, and allows your reader to find your sources easily.

The mistake some students make is to think that the words of experts sound smarter than their own, so they are tempted to "borrow" them without citing the source. Whether you are stealing directly or paraphrasing without citing your source, this is known as **plagiarism**, implying that these are your words, your thoughts, when they really belong to someone else. Ironically, if you find experts to back up your ideas, quote them and cite the source—*that's* what makes you sound smart! As far as finding your own voice, trust the process; committed practice will make it happen.

10. Revising and editing.

Interviewer: How much rewriting do you do?

Hemingway: It depends. I rewrote the ending of *Farewell to Arms*, the last page of it, 39 times before I was satisfied.

Interviewer: Was there some technical problem there? What was it that had stumped you?

Hemingway: Getting the words right.

(Ernest Hemingway, "The Art of Fiction No. 21," *The Paris Review*, interview by George Plimpton, 1958)

No essay is nearly complete after one draft. Most writers and successful students agree that good writing is about 10 per cent writing and 90 per cent revision. An essay consists of content and form; both are necessary. It is only in the revision process, once your rough ideas are down on paper that you can step back and concentrate on form: not *what* you are saying, rather *how* well you are saying it. After one draft, you have the clay, but not yet the sculpture. Now you must craft, shape, polish, and polish again. This is the process of acquiring style. Its purpose is a refinement, clarity of thought and expression. This text endeavors to help you in that process.

It is always best to revise a day or two after you've completed a draft. Allow yourself enough time to get some distance from the creative process, so you can approach the draft with a critical eye. Revise first, then edit. In revision, you critically review the overall shape and logic of organization, paragraphs, and sentences; in editing, you look at the fine detail, conventions such as spelling, punctuation, grammar. Now is also the opportunity to "turn a phrase" through word choice, figures of speech, patterns of repetition, and such that make reading a delight.

Read through your essay slowly, as many times as needed, using the following:

Revision Checklist

- Does the title state my main idea precisely, and does it capture my reader's interest?
- Does the thesis statement clearly reflect what I achieve in the body of the essay?
- Does the essay have a clearly defined beginning, middle, and end?
- Is each paragraph unified; that is, one main idea, developed, and supported?
- Are my paragraphs in the most effective order? Do they flow logically?

- Did I use a variety of sentence types for interest? (see lessons 9–14, 17)
- Is my language concise and precise? (see lesson 24).
  - Avoid any unnecessary or redundant words (true fact, past history).
  - Avoid wordy constructions (due to the fact that—use—because). Thomas Jefferson said, "*The most valuable of all talents is that of never using two words when one will do.*"
  - Can two or more ideas be joined in a compound or complex sentence?
- Did I lazily use scaffolding? Avoid phrases such as "This essay will prove . . . ." or "This shows that . . . ." or "This quotation means or shows . . . ." These phrases are always unnecessary. Simply state your point.
- Is my language sufficiently formal? Remember not to use intensives (amazing, incredible). Don't use contractions (don't, it's, aren't). Avoid clichés, slang, jargon or informal abbreviations (OMG). Have I shown that I can write well, notwithstanding my ideas?
- Are there any punctuation, spelling or grammatical errors? These kinds of errors will put your English instructor in a negative frame of mind because there is no need for carelessness. And the conventions matter. In Isaac Babel's story "Guy de Maupassant," the narrator states: "No iron can pierce the heart with such force as a period put just at the right place." He was talking about fiction, but this also holds true for essay writing. Keep a list of errors you frequently make so that you can edit for them in all your essays.
- Do all my pronouns (he, she, it) have an antecedent? Avoid starting sentences with "It" or "This" as much as possible. Always try to use the noun you are referring to instead. However, if you do use a pronoun make sure it refers directly to a noun. (see Handbook of Style and Grammar Terms 127.)
- Did I use the third person point of view? Do not use "I" or "you" for a formal essay unless for a specific reason or request from a professor.
- Did I use the active voice? Avoid the passive whenever possible. In the active voice the subject acts: *The student wrote the essay.* In the passive voice the pattern is reversed and the subject is acted upon: *The essay was written by the student.* The use of "was" is the clue here. The passive voice always includes some form of the verb "to be." It is wordy and, well, passive. The active voice is more concise, direct and dynamic. (see Handbook of Style and Grammar Terms 127)
- Is my tone appropriate? E.B White said, "*No one can write decently who is distrustful of the reader's intelligence or whose attitude is patronizing.*" Tone (see Handbook of Style and Grammar Terms 127) is unavoidable; it happens whether you craft it or not, so use it to your advantage.

Ideally, one must strike the right balance: objective, engaging, measured, confident but modest. Reading your essay out loud to a friend will allow you to hear your tone. (see lesson 18)

- Did I use the present tense for the base tense? Is the verb tense consistent throughout the essay? (see Handbook of Style and Grammar Terms 127)

- Did I speculate, ramble or pad? Be very specific and in interpretive essays take information principally from the text itself. Avoid tangential, unnecessary or unsubstantiated pronouncements. Instead, argue your precise contention.

- Is my writing alive? Does it dance across the page or sag like a heavy weight? Can I improve it with better word choice—starting with verbs?

- Did I follow the guidelines for my chosen documenting style (MLA, APA, Chicago)? Is the essay double spaced from beginning to end? Do not add space between paragraphs, simply indent.

- LOOK IT UP. If you are uncertain of a spelling or a grammatical rule or the format for citing, do not use an approximation; do not tell yourself "it will do." It will not do if you want a good grade.

- Finally, read your essay out loud, listening for any awkwardness, gaps, or stumbling blocks. Often you can hear problems that you can't see. Better still—get a friend to read it to you. You will hear even more, especially when they stumble or look puzzled. Revise until you are proud of it.

- After all that hard work, don't baulk at your grade: learn from it. Find out what you can do to make the essay better next time. Writing is an art, a craft, and a reflection of your intellectual and creative skills. There are no shortcuts, but the long-term rewards for persistent work are truly satisfying. Start early and give it your best.

Your grades will improve in exact proportion to the care you give the whole writing process. Allow yourself enough time to collect material, to think, out-line, research, write a draft, revise and edit. One long, late night will not suffice. The essay is the major evaluation tool in the university; give it the time and attention it needs.

Finally, don't be afraid to ask for help. If there is something you don't understand, see your instructor, and use the many writing and grammar texts in the reference section of the library. If you are having difficulties, then find a writing lab where you can receive individual attention. Writing is a learned skill; there are people waiting to help. All you have to do is ask.

Part Four

Handbook of Style and Grammar Terms

Allusion

An allusion is a brief reference to something well-known and assumed to be understood by both writer and reader, such as an historical, mythical, or literary person, place, event, or object. Allusions are used in many art forms to enrich the artist's message. How would you interpret the following allusion to the biblical character Jonas who, having disobeyed God, was swallowed by a whale:

> "Fiction was invented the day Jonas arrived home and told his wife that he was three days late because he had been swallowed by a whale." (Gabriel Garcia Marquez)

Look how brilliant this example is. On first reading, we think—right, Jonah told a story, that is, a fib; Marquez is being satirical, even cynical, and fiction is an invention, a lie. Then we realize—wait, no, Jonah was truly in the belly of the whale for three days and three nights; he tells his wife the truth, and she is drawn in and held spellbound, like the Ancient Mariner's wedding guest, to his incredible tale. Of course, that is an interpretation, and you might have a different one. But to form an opinion, first you must recognize the allusion. The more you know about the object or event alluded to, the more deeply you will understand the allusion.

But Jonas isn't the only source of allusion in this quotation. Marquez is working on many levels; he also alludes, subtly, to a complex and long-standing argument about the nature of fiction. He plays on not the pattern of repetition itself, but the idea of *ploche* or *polyptoton*—a pattern of repetition in which a word is repeated in a different form. Here, Marquez questions the meaning of *story* as "fib" compared to story as "the invention of truth." You might wonder, *isn't that an oxymoron: "invented truth"*? Most fiction writers maintain that their inventions (fictions) express a truth about the world and the human condition. The question is *does that make the stories "true"*? You can see that we are involved in another *polyptoton—truth/true*, which plays on the connotations of *true/real* and *true/authentic*. Fiction writers argue that something does not necessarily have to be *true* to tell a *truth*. On the other side of the argument, Plato wanted to throw the poets out of the ideal society because these inventions, he held, were thrice removed from reality and therefore not trustworthy. However, the jury is still out.

Parody

Parody, a form of commentary often used by comedians, involves elements of allusion. This following example is from the Victorian music hall comedian Dan Leno:

> "Ah! What is man? Wherefore does he why? Whence does he whence? Whither is he whithering?"

The humour resides not only in the play of language, but also in the play on allusions—the parody. Parody is the act of making fun of something by imitating words, style, tone, or ideas. Leno is alluding to the three questions composer Johannes Brahms told his students to ask of "the Maker" for inspiration—*wherefore, whence, whither*—or to Paul Gauguin's famous Tahiti painting: *Where do we come from? What are we? Where are we going?* It rings of Shakespeare: "*What a piece of work is man!*" ("Hamlet" 2.2) There are also essays throughout history entitled "What is Man?"—a title that Leno alludes to at the beginning, upping the ante of seriousness, so that, in parody, each play on language is funnier than the last.

Appositives

Apposition means placing side by side, juxtaposition. An appositive is a word, phrase, or clause that restates the subject immediately in the sentence construction, to expand, identify, modify, or clarify the subject. Because it is efficient and effective, it is often used in academic writing.

Non-restrictive appositives (use commas)

Because a non-restrictive appositive adds information to the subject, but is not essential to the meaning of the main clause, it is treated like an aside. Place commas on both sides of the appositive:

Phil Fontaine, *past national chief of Canada's First Nations*, was born in 1944.

A non-restrictive appositive often interrupts the main clause:

The winner, *a young woman from Ethiopia*, sailed over the finish line well ahead of the others.

Identify the appositives in the following entry from the on-line *Canadian Encyclopedia*. Can you make this entry both more efficient and more effective by using more appositives, or is there a limit to this device's use?:

There are 2 commercial types of mica: muscovite (potassium mica) and phlogopite (magnesium mica). Muscovite, the mica with the greatest commercial use, is an important constituent of granite and the main constituent of some schists. It is usually colourless, but may be green or light yellow, or transparent. It is very resistant to chemical and thermal attack. Because it has high electrical resistivity and dielectric strength, muscovite sheet mica (large flat sheets that can be cut or stamped into required shapes) is used as an insulator in electrical and electronic equipment. Its many uses include lasers, pyrometers, radar systems, missile systems, and aerospace components.

Restrictive clauses

Appositives that are essential to the main idea of the sentence do not take commas:

> "No one *who had ever seen Catherine Morland in her infancy* would have supposed her born to be a heroine." (Jane Austen, *Northanger Abbey*)

> The idea *that Plato threw the poets out of the ideal society* still haunts modern writers.

Rules of thumb: *who/that, that/which*

Use the functional relative *who* for people and *that* for anything non-human. Use the functional relative *that* for restrictive clauses (no commas) and *which* for non-restrictive clauses (with commas). As with any rule, there are always exceptions. Note how brilliantly James Joyce breaks the comma rules in the following quotation:

> "Pain, *that was not yet the pain of love*, fretted his heart." (*Ulysses*)

Joyce's use of *that* suggests a restrictive clause, in which case it should not take commas. If he had used *which*, it would have taken commas. There are, of course, instances where writers will use *that* where they should use *which* simply out of carelessness, but I don't think this is one of them. By using *that* with the commas, Joyce presents the clause simultaneously as a restrictive clause and as an aside. This is a contradiction, so why would he? It throws the emphasis on the aside. (Read the sentence without commas or with *which*.) The *that* signals that the aside is in fact a restrictive clause; at the same time, the commas instinctively slow us down; they make us breathe the sentence differently. But this is not all Joyce does to throw emphasis here. The periodic nature of the clause also creates tension and rhythm. Do you hear the arc of the sentence? That arc also creates the tender ache of it. Did Joyce do all this consciously, deliberately? It is possible that he did not, at least not when he first wrote the sentence. But at some point, probably during the editing process, the good writer will make a deliberate choice.

Clauses

A clause is a group of words with a subject and a finite verb. There are two kinds of clauses: *independent* and *dependent*.

Independent clauses

An independent clause consists of one subject/verb connection; it is a complete thought, which can stand on its own. A simple sentence, therefore, can be thought of as an independent clause. However, when we speak of independent clauses, we are generally referring to clauses that contribute to more complex structures, such as compound or complex sentences. For example, consider the following two independent clauses joined by parataxis:

> s/v   s/v
> "*We are* never deceived; *we deceive* ourselves." (Johann Wolfgang von Goethe)

In complex sentences the main (independent) clause can be:

- placed at the beginning of the sentence (called a loose sentence);
- placed in the centre of the sentence (a centred sentence);
- placed at the end of the sentence (a periodic sentence); and/or
- interrupted by another clause (a convoluted sentence).

Independent clauses are joined using one of four devices: coordinating conjunctions, correlative conjunctions, parataxis, or conjunctive adverbs.

Coordinating conjunctions
The most commonly used coordinating conjunctions are *and, but, for, or, nor, so,* and *yet*. Coordinating conjunctions reveal specific relationships, so choose carefully. A coordinating conjunction is preceded by a comma when it joins two independent clauses. (see also **conjunctions**)

Correlative conjunctions
Correlative conjunctions always appear in pairs. They include *either/or, neither/nor, not only/but also,* and *both/and*. (see also **conjunctions**)

Parataxis
Parataxis involves using only a semicolon (or a comma, if you are joining two short sentences). This method works best when the relationship between the two clauses is obvious. It is more emphatic than the other methods and draws a sharper contrast between the elements it connects.

Conjunctive adverbs
Conjunctive adverbs include *also, besides, consequently, for example, furthermore, in addition, moreover, nevertheless, otherwise, similarly, still, therefore,* and *thus*. In this method, a semicolon precedes the conjunctive adverb and a comma follows it.

Dependent clauses
A dependent clause also consists of one subject/verb connection, but the dependent clause is subordinated to the main clause by a subordinating conjunction. The subordinating conjunction makes it an incomplete thought; therefore, a dependent clause is never found alone.

```
              main clause                    subordinate clause
         s/v                          conj.              s/v
    "The lonely one offers his hand too quickly to whomever he encounters."
```
(Friedrich Nietzsche, *Thus Spoke Zarathustra*)

A dependent clause always acts as a grammatical part of the sentence. There are *noun clauses, adjectival clauses,* and *adverbial clauses.*

Consider the following famous quotations from Nietzsche:

```
       dependent noun clause   independent (main) clause
    sub. conj.   s/v                  s/v
    "What does not destroy me makes me strong." (Twilight of the Idols)
```

What does not destroy me is a noun clause acting as the subject of the main clause. *What* is the subordinating conjunction, a functional relative that also acts as the subject in the subordinating clause.

```
          independent                      dependent adjectival
       s/v        c. conj.          (c. conj.: that)           s/v
    "God is dead; but considering the state the species of man is in,
       independent                            dependent adjectival
       s/v                          s. conj.              s/v
    there will perhaps be caves, for ages yet, in which his shadow will be
    shown." (The Gay Science)
```

This is a compound-complex sentence. The compound sentence consists of two independent clauses: *God is dead (but) there will perhaps be caves.* The complex sentence adds on two subordinate clauses: *[that] the species of man is in* (modifying *considering the state*) and *in which his shadow will be shown* (modifying *caves*).

Restrictive and non-restrictive clauses

A *restrictive clause* is essential to the meaning of the sentence. It cannot be removed without changing the meaning—it restricts the meaning; therefore, it *does not* take commas.

> "A person *who publishes a book* appears willfully in public with his pants down." (Edna St. Vincent Millay)

> "One of the advantages of being disorderly is *that one is constantly making exciting discoveries.*" (A.A. Milne)

A *non-restrictive clause* is not essential to the meaning of the sentence. Think of it as an aside, a parenthetical thought, something added to the sentence that can be removed without changing the essential meaning; therefore, it *does* take commas:

"Tides in the Minas Basin, *into which the Shubenacadie River flows*, rise and fall 13 metres on average and more than 16 metres during spring tides when the sun and moon are aligned to exert a maximum pull on the waters of the Earth. These are the highest tides in the world." (Harry Thurston, *Tidal Life*)

(See also **appositives**, particularly, the **rules of thumb** for *who/that* and *that/which*.)

Diction

Diction requires *choosing* your words, rather than merely accepting whatever pops into your head. In a letter to his student, Guy Maupassant, Gustave Flaubert made the following analysis:

"Whatever you want to say, there is only one word to express it; one verb to make it move, one adjective to qualify it. You must seek that word, that verb, that adjective and never be satisfied with approximations, never resort to tricks, even clever ones, or to verbal sleight of hands to escape a difficulty."

There are several kinds of "approximations." The first involves Flaubert's dictum—that you must find the precise word; for example, the word *walked* tells us little, it is an approximation, but *lumbered* is precise. The second involves using tired expressions to avoid the work of choosing precise words, or using clichés instead of creating your own metaphors. But there is a third sense in which we use approximations, and end up writing imprecisely, and this has to do with accuracy. For example, I am writing an email to a friend, forwarding a request from an organization I deeply respect. I begin the email by writing "I never forward these requests, but I thought this one worthwhile." *Never* is imprecise—an approximation only. To be accurate I should say, depending on the truth, "I have never before . . . ." or "I seldom . . . ." Revising for precision is more than surfing for a word; it requires thinking deeply about meaning.

Ellipsis

An ellipsis refers to any deliberate grammatical omission in the structure of the sentence.

One form of ellipsis is the three spaced periods to show omission, as in the following quotation, where I have omitted an appositive from a sentence in Terry Eagleton's *Literary Theory*:

What was specific to literary language . . . was that it deformed ordinary language in various ways. Under the pressure of literary devices, ordinary language was intensified, condensed, twisted, telescoped, drawn out, turned on its head. It was language "made strange"; and because of this estrangement, the everyday world was also suddenly made unfamiliar.

Notice that the sentence is grammatically correct despite the ellipsis.

Ellipsis also refers to a writer's choice to omit words that are not necessary to complete the meaning of a sentence. Consider the following examples:

Original: He is running the marathon; she is running the half marathon. When they are ready, they sign in and are given their numbers. She is faster than the other competitors are.

Using ellipses: He is running the marathon, she the half marathon. When ready, they sign in and are given their numbers. She is faster than her competitors.

It would be unwise to use an ellipsis if it blurred or confused meaning. However, where the words are not necessary to complete the sense, an ellipsis increases concision.

Emphatic Devices

Emphatic devices are used to draw attention to a word, phrase, clause, or sentence. These devices can involve addition (accumulation, appositives), subtraction (ellipses), interruption, position, repetition, or transposition (isolation, inversion). Emphatic devices are subtler and more sophisticated than devices of *mechanical emphasis*, which include underlining, italics, and exclamation marks. The devices examined in this handbook to style and grammar do not by any means exhaust the list, but they are the most common. You will notice how these devices are often used in combinations, and so overlap, enhancing and reinforcing one another. For each device listed below, I have included an illustrative quotation; I have also embedded an example in each definition itself—see if you can find it.

Accumulation

Accumulation refers to the use of words, phrases, or clauses piled up in a sentence to draw attention. They include paired adjectives, piled participial phrases (see lesson 9), and piled clauses (see lesson 27). The knack in creating potent and persuasive accumulation is to use your ear as your guide. It is worth knowing that English writers traditionally have had a preference for grammatical units piled in twos or threes. But you can use any number to create the effect you want. Make sure that the accumulation has a purpose, and use it sparingly. Remember that individually paired and piled words—adjectives, verbs, adverbs, nouns—*must* be in a parallel construction. Piled phrases and clauses do not *need* to take grammatically identical forms, but they are most pleasing to the ear if they too are in parallel construction:

The yolk of a turtle egg cooks readily into a soft, mushy yellow. The albumen, though, *pops and bubbles and jumps* around the pan, and will not congeal. No matter how blazing the heat beneath it may be, the white of the egg of the snapping turtle will not *turn milky and set*. It will jump like a frog, *and bounce and dance and skitter* all over the pan until *your patience snaps or the fire dies.* So you give up trying to cook it. You swallow it *hot and raw.* (John McPhee, "Travels in Georgia," *The New Yorker*)

Ellipsis

As an emphatic device, *ellipsis* refers to the omission of words necessary to complete the grammar of a sentence, but not the meaning. We find this device in writing, but more frequently in speech. Whether or not we are fully aware of it, with an ellipsis, we supply the missing words for ourselves:

The writing is almost as good as Dillard's.

The writing is almost as good as Dillard's (writing is).

Find the ellipsis in the following quotation by the humorist P.G. Wodehouse:

"It's a good idea never to apologize. The right sort of people do not want apologies, and the wrong sort take a mean advantage of them."

Ellipsis, if used cautiously, can improve concision, but you must tread a fine line:

"The only way round is through." (Robert Frost)

Frost's quotation makes us think deeply about what is missing; because of the ellipsis, there are levels of meaning, both literal and symbolic. However, there are few places in formal writing where the reader will welcome this degree of opacity. When using ellipsis, always check that it improves concision without losing clarity. Also, be careful not to use ellipsis in writing as often as we do in speech.

(For ellipsis as omission, see also the previous entry for **ellipsis**.)

Interruption

Interruption involves interrupting the main clause with a word or a word group. This emphatic device, often overlapping with isolation, applies to sentences where the effect emphasizes the whole idea, rather than a word or phrase:

"Education today, *more than ever before,* must see clearly its dual objectives: educating for living and educating for making a living." (James Mason Wood)

"Many plays, *certainly mine,* are like blank cheques. The actors and directors put their own signatures on them." (Thornton Wilder)

Inversion

Inversion, used most often for emphasis, inverts or changes the natural word order:

"*About suffering,* they were never wrong, *the old masters.*" (W.H. Auden, "Musée des Beaus Arts")

Inversion may overlap with interruption:

"The past, *at least*, is secure." (Daniel Webster, "Second Speech on Foot's Resolution")

Isolation

Isolation refers to a word (usually) or phrase set off from the rest of the sentence, or out of its usual order. This device draws attention to the isolated word(s):

Desperately, he eyed the tundra's expansive, unobstructed horizon for any sign of life.

Isolation often occurs at the beginning or end of the sentence, but not necessarily so. The word(s) can also be isolated in the middle of a sentence by the use of punctuation: a set of dashes, a question mark, parenthesis, or a colon:

He eyed the tundra's expansive, unobstructed horizon—*desperately*—for any sign of life.

Parallel construction

Parallel constructions are not only efficient and pleasing to the ear, they can also aid in emphasis. They refer to words, phrases, clauses, or sentences that share an exact grammatical pattern. The construction is emphatic primarily because the repetition of the construction significantly aids in memory and understanding:

"If my theory of relativity is proven correct, Germany will claim me as a German and France will declare that I am a citizen of the world. Should my theory prove untrue, France will say that I am a German, and Germany will declare that I am a Jew." (Albert Einstein, in *The Times*, London)

However, not all parallel constructions are inherently emphatic. For example, lists are not necessarily so:

My list for the day read brush the dog, do the laundry, write my thesis.

The parallel construction is efficient, concise, pleasing to the ear, but does it alone draw our attention? What is working with parallel construction, in Einstein's quotation, to create a memorable effect?

What about the following example:

My list for the day reads: sell my dog, burn my laundry, write my thesis.

This is a parallel construction. Each of the phrases has the same grammatical pattern: (infinitive) verb, (possessive) adjective, and noun. But what really draws our attention? Two other devices conjoin with the parallel construction to make the sentence emphatic: the use of the colon and the use of irony (saying one thing but meaning another). The colon acts as an announcement, throwing emphasis on the list (as if to say "here comes something important"). The irony—residing in the unlikelihood of selling the dog or burning the laundry, thus implying that writing the thesis in a day is also unlikely but probably the source of the problem—is the final device; it helps to crystallize the meaning of the sentence. Form and content work together, form enhancing meaning.

Position

In constructing complex sentences, there are three positions where you may choose to place the main clause: beginning, middle, or end. Two of these positions (beginning and end) are emphatic, the end position being the most emphatic.

This also holds true for words and phrases within a sentence. The beginning and end of a sentence are the most emphatic positions, unless you use another emphatic device such as isolation, inversion, or mechanical emphasis in the middle. For example, putting your subject in the opening position enhances clarity by getting right to the point:

"An intellectual is someone whose mind watches itself." (Albert Camus, *Notebooks*)

"Biography is history seen through a prism of a person." (Louis Fischer)

This position can also enhance a contrast:

"The young feel tired at the end of an action; the old at the beginning." (T.S. Eliot, *Murder in the Cathedral*)

Note also Eliot's use of the ellipsis.

The end position is used to create tension, to raise curiosity, and to enhance memory. In the following quotation, the idea of the main clause is not completed until the very last word:

"You cannot be friends upon any other terms than upon the terms of equality." (Woodrow Wilson, Address before the Southern Commercial Congress in Mobile Alabama, 1913.)

Punctuation

Emphatic punctuation includes the colon and dash, when used to isolate or for announcement; the exclamation point; and the question mark, when used in the middle of a sentence. These forms of punctuation are seldom used in formal essay writing except when the writer is constructing an announcement. *Announcement* refers to the use of a dash or colon (or sometimes a comma) to announce—here comes something important: a list, the main idea, or an appositive.

"Chesterton taught me this: the only way to be sure of catching a train is to miss the one before it." (Pierre Daninos, *Vacances a tous prix*)

The comma is least emphatic; the dash more emphatic; the colon most emphatic. Use a colon where you want to directly introduce or announce a word, phrase, clause, or list. Notice that there are other places in this definition where I might have used a colon, but I did not want to overwhelm the paragraph with too many. The longer stops—a dash, semicolon, and colon—are top heavy, and you must be wary of toppling a sentence or paragraph by over use. This is especially true in poetry.

Repetition

Repetition includes the deliberate repetition of letters (such as alliteration, assonance, and consonance), words, phrases, clauses, and ideas. Given their usefulness, it is odd that except for the first category—letters—the patterns of repetition are seldom taught in school. Their effective employment is one of the ways we can distinguish great writers from mediocre writers.

Most writers nowadays must discover these devices on their own or use them intuitively. The patterns of repetition were first set down by the ancient Greeks (which explains their unpronounceable names), but modern writers are probably more indebted to Henry Peacham's text, *The Garden of Eloquence*, published in 1577 and revised in 1593, in which Peacham defines and illustrates 184 rhetorical devices.

You will find a list and description of commonly used patterns in the *Canadian Oxford Guide to Writing*, and there are some excellent websites dedicated to a discussion of these devices. As the *Canadian Oxford Guide to Writing* points out—it is not the Greek label that is important, but the pattern of repetition itself, so concentrate on understanding the definition rather than memorizing the label.

Here, we will take a closer look at some of the more common devices. Each of the following six patterns describe ways in which the same word can be repeated for emphasis.

Anaphora

Anaphora is the repetition of the same word or words at the beginning of successive clauses or phrases. You'll find anaphora everywhere, most noticeably in great oration, political speeches, advertising, and even the movies:

"Of all the gin joints, in all the towns, in all the world, she walks into mine." (the character Rick Blaine in the movie "Casablanca")

Anaphora is often associated with clauses, as in Martin Luther King Jr's famous "I have a dream" speech, in which eight sentences in a row begin with the clause "I have a dream." But anaphora is also effective in phrases, as in these three participial phrases from Barbara Gowdy's short story "Body and Soul":

> "What wins Aunt Bea's heart is the sight of those two wing-like arms *flapping at one of her artificial arms* (she insists on putting them on her herself), *flapping and failing to grasp it, flapping and falling*, and at last lining it up, slipping the stump into the socket, and clicking it in."

Diacope

Diacope is the repetition of a word or words separated by one or two other words.

> "Not necessarily conscription, but conscription if necessary." (William Lyon Mackenzie King)

> "It's no use trying to be clever—we are all clever here; just try to be kind—a little kind." (Dr. Foakes Jackson, said to a new don at Jesus College in Cambridge)

Epistrophe

Epistrophe is the repetition of the same word or words at the end of successive clauses or phrases.

> "When I came back to Dublin, I was court-martialled in my absence, and sentenced to death in my absence, so I said they could shoot me in my absence." (Brendan Behan, *The Hostage*)

The following quotation uses both anaphora and epistrophe:

> "What lies behind us and what lies before us are tiny compared to what lies within us." (Ralph Waldo Emerson)

Epizeuxis

Epizeuxis is the immediate repetition of a word. This pattern is tricky to use. You can easily end up sounding didactic or too old fashion: *It was a fine, fine day.* Yet look how George Elliott Clarke makes it work in his novel *George & Rue*:

> "Their childhood was cups of grease on a battered table; rat poison set out carefully, carefully, like meals fit for kings; hailstorms wiping out any pretty good crop; lovely heavy crops reduced to blotches by too much water; a horde of hail and a flood of rain carrying off everything."

Note that Clarke also uses diacope (*crops*).

Polyptoton

Polyptoton is the repetition of a word in a different form.

> "Sanity in a world of insanity is insane." (R.D. Laing)

See also William Lyon Mackenzie King's quotation above, under "Diacope" (*necessarily/necessary*).

Tautotes

Tautotes is the repetition of a word two or more times:

> "From this youngest son's failure to dog-paddle the father saw other failures multiply like an explosion of virulent cells—failure to speak clearly; failure to sit up straight; failure to get up in the morning; failure in attitude; failure in ambition and ability; indeed, in everything. His own failure." (Annie Proulx, *The Shipping News*)

Let's take a closer look at this quotation: the first two repetitions are a (slight) polyptoton (*failure/failures*) and the next five are an anaphora. You might wonder how tautotes differs from diacope or epizeuxis or polyptoton or anaphora. It doesn't, necessarily. Think of tautotes as an umbrella term that covers examples (for example, that last *failure*) that do not fit into any of the other patterns.

Rhyme, rhythm, and cadence

Rhyme

Broadly speaking, rhyme refers to the repetition of sound. There are many forms (masculine, feminine, assonance, consonance, internal rhyme, end rhyme) used by the poet; but good prose writers also use some forms of rhyme. The difference is that, in prose, the rhyme should be less obtrusive—the reader should not be fully aware of the rhyme, nor should the rhyme be in any way awkward or unwittingly used—what is referred to as "unfortunate rhyme." Like the modern poet, the prose writer uses rhyme primarily for emphasis and to enhance rhythm. A prose writer seldom uses perfect rhyme, that is, an exact correspondence to the vowel and following consonants: *room/doom; still/frill*. It is too obvious, too blatant. Prose writers will, however, use imperfect rhyme (also known as partial or slant rhyme) to draw attention. In partial rhyme, either the vowel or the final consonants are similar rather than identical. Partial rhyme is favoured by the modern poet, who is closer to the modern prose writer than earlier poets in this regard. The modern poet selects a combination of rhyme and rhythm—usually avoiding blatant devices like iambic pentameter and end rhyme. As an example, consider the following poem, which I have included from my unpublished works:

> **Dusk**
> *Andante*
> the sun sinks below the clouds
> bathes the birch, gilds its leaves,
> hovers there, burns scarlet,
> crimson, tangerine
> it turns heads, stops the hand

a quietude descends diminishing
the cacophony of human sounds,
bird song, even the wind; into
this tranquility, this vespertine retreat
the world enters, breathes, darkens,
slips into silence, nakedness, divine
vulnerability.

What makes this language poetic? What gives it its movement? It's not a traditional form—not a sonnet—and it doesn't have a set meter. There is very little perfect rhyme and no end rhyme. But there is a wealth of other forms, which include alliteration (*s, b, d*) and partial rhyme (*hand/sounds, wind/into, leaves/breathes*—although *leaves* and *breathes* are far apart in the poem, the rhyme resounds because the e sound is pulled through the poem). Modern poets and prose writers will use this method of rhyme wherein a particular sound (vowel or consonant) is repeated, not as deliberate end rhyme, but as internal rhyme (inside the line). Notice how other sounds are pulled through the poem (the short *i* as in *sink, crimson, it, diminishing, wind, into, tranquility, slips*, and *vulnerability*) and the letter s both in the starting and ending position of the words.

Good prose writers will use poetic techniques in moderation to create a variety of moods—from haunting to lyrical—in their writing. The question is: how much can the prose writer get away with? Look at the following example from Annie Dillard's *For the Time Being*, which explains where sand comes from—not what you might think of as a particularly poetic topic. See if you can identify the poetic devices Dillard employs:

Mostly, the continents' streams and rivers make sand. Streams, especially, and fast rivers bear bouncing rocks that knock the earth, and break themselves into sharp chips of sand. The sand grains leap—saltate—downstream. So the banks and bottoms of most streams are sandy. Look in any small stream in the woods or mountains, as far inland as you like. That stream is making sand, and sand lies on its bed.

Rhythm

Rhythm in writing refers to the sound, the pacing, the movement of the prose. As a writer, you might try to ignore this aspect of your writing, but, like style, it will still be there whether you attend to it or not. Rhythm is a significant component of good writing.

Aaron Copland, in *What to Listen for in Music*, states that the earliest music of which we have any record "invariably accompanied prose or poetry as a modest handmaiden. From the Greeks to the full flowering of the Gregorian chant the rhythm of music was the natural, unfettered rhythm of prose or poetic speech. No one then, or since, has been able to write down that kind of rhythm with any degree of exactitude" (32). It wasn't until music became more regulated that it was successfully transcribed.

This note is interesting because that earlier *untranscribable* rhythm is what we are talking about. The more obvious the rhythm is in writing, the more attention it draws, the more emphatic it becomes. What the good writer hopes to achieve rhythmically in a text is similar to what a composer strives for in a composition: a pleasing sound with a variety of beats and stresses, creating a variety of moods, bound together by some thread—a motif or theme—that flows from beginning to end. Think of paragraphs as movements in a sonata—you would not want them all the same, yet there needs to be something integral that holds them together. Artists do this in both music and writing, in part, by repeating a particular rhythm, varying a recognizable rhythm, and orchestrating the pace and movement of the rhythm.

Since it has early manifestations in speech patterns, one way to improve your rhythm is to read your prose out loud, listening for flaws: awkwardness, interrupted flow, monotony, flatness, too much activity (variety), or loss of emphasis. If your ear detects a weakness, think about how you have (or have not) used variety in sentence patterns and lengths, parallel constructions, units of two or three, repetition, and accumulation. All of these devices help shape the movement of the prose—the rhythm.

As an aside, you should note that meter and rhythm are related, but not the same thing. People who read measured poetry, particularly poetry that has end rhyme, by the meter are ignoring the natural rhythm that adheres to the *meaning*, not the meter. In poetry this is one of the tensions that creates pleasure—when you must read the meaning against the meter.

Cadence

In music, *cadence* refers to "the resolution at the end a musical phrase"; in rhythm, it means "the measure or beat of sound or movement"; in speech, it means the rise and fall "of the voice, especially at the end of a phrase"; more broadly, it means tonal inflection (*Canadian Oxford Dictionary* 212). In writing, therefore, we use the word cadence to mean the rise and fall, the tonal inflection, of the inner voice reading the words. How do you improve your cadence? By practice. By reading your work aloud and listening carefully to its measure, its beat, the rise and fall as it moves toward the denouement of each sentence and paragraph. Reading good writers—especially great writers—aloud will improve your ear for cadence and give you patterns to emulate.

Sentence styles

In the lessons, we discussed a number of sentence styles—the short simple sentence, the freight train, the triad, the fragment—that can be used for a variety of effects, including emphasis.

The imperative sentence (see lesson 6) draws the reader's attention because it lacks a subject. If used sparingly, it can create a powerful effect in academic writing.

To review, identify the emphatic devices that are at work in the following title of the poem by Herbert Trench:

"Come, let us make Love deathless."

(See also **sentences**.)

Figurative Language

The broadest definition for the term *figurative language* refers to any use of language that deviates from the literal meaning of a group of words:

"If a man empties his purse into his head, no one can take it from him."
(Ben Franklin)

How might you restate Franklin's thought without the use of metaphor?

M.H. Abrams defines figurative language as "a conspicuous departure from what users of a language apprehend as the standard meaning of words, or else the standard order of words, in order to achieve some special meaning or effect" (96). He delineates two types: figures of thought (tropes) and figures of speech. However, not all theorists agree with this distinction. For our purposes, we will simply call them "figures" and examine six commonly used figures: simile, metaphor, analogy, allegory, symbol, and personification. Think of the first four figures as comparisons—each of these becoming more complex.

If you want to develop your ability to use effective figurative language, you must practise. At the end of the day, use whatever you have studied or experienced to try to create figurative language. Even studying grammar provides vehicles; for example: *a good marriage is like a compound rather than a complex sentence, the two are of equal weight, equal significance.*

Simile

A simile is a direct comparison between two distinctly different things that have something in common.

"A child like your stomach doesn't need all you can afford to give it."
(Frank A. Clark)

"Pro football is like nuclear warfare. There are no winners, only survivors."
(Frank Gifford)

Similes usually use *like* or *as* to connect the two things being compared, but you could use others words—such as *akin to*—or you might just suggest a simile:

"My two favorite things in life are libraries and bicycles. They both move people forward without wasting anything." (Peter Golkin)

Metaphor

A metaphor is an indirect comparison between two distinctly different things. An *implicit metaphor* is one in which the subject or tenor is not actually stated, but rather implied.

In *Text Book: An Introduction to Literary Language*, Scholes, Comley and Ulmer define metaphor as a process, arguing that "in a metaphor the name of one thing is applied to another so that, as in certain chemical reactions, there is an exchange of particles between the two" (46). Their example is: "words are razor blades" (46). When we compare words to razor blades, certain attributes of razor blades are transferred to words—namely, delicate, and dangerous. Metaphor is not an ornament added on top of language, but rather a principle built in at the most fundamental level of language (46), a way for us to understand elements of our reality in relation to one another. A metaphor lives when it brings to mind more than a single reference and the several references are seen to have something in common (52). A metaphor dies (a dead metaphor or cliché) when we no longer make the comparison, or when the writer constructs so surreal a comparison that the two referents simply do not have anything in common (53). Metaphors should be unexpected but appropriate (57).

Metaphor is not the exclusive tool of literature. It is used powerfully in all types of writing, as in the following excerpt from a speech given by Elizabeth Cady Stanton in 1892, one of the opening gambits of women's suffrage in America. Note Stanton's use of the *extended metaphor* of a voyage:

> The strongest reason why we ask for woman a voice in the government under which she lives; in the religion she is asked to believe; equality in social life, where she is the chief factor; a place in the trades and professions, where she may earn her bread, is because of her birthright to self-sovereignty; because, as an individual, she must rely on herself. No matter how much women prefer to lean, to be protected and supported, nor how much men desire to have them do so, they must make the voyage of life alone, and for safety in an emergency they must know something of the laws of navigation. To guide our own craft, we must be captain, pilot, engineer; with chart and compass to stand at the wheel; to match the wind and waves and know when to take in the sail, and to read the signs in the firmament over all. It matters not whether the solitary voyager is man or woman.

Re-examine the similes. Can they be turned into metaphors? In each case, which device works best? Why?

Cliché

Clichés are dead metaphors—metaphors so over used that we have stopped making the comparison. Because they deaden writing, clichés should be avoided.

Of course, good writers can break any rule. Look at this use of a cliché by Karen Gordon in her remarkable book *The Deluxe Transitive Vampire*:

> "He knew suffering from inside out, abjection like the back of his hand, which was slender and silken and thrilling to all who were touched by him."

Gordon takes the cliché of "knowing something like the back of your hand" and forces us to revisit this tired expression in a new light. She makes the connection by describing the back of the vampire's hand, which is not as we would expect—an ironic little joke on the reader. She draws our attention with the use of alliteration, piled adjectives, and polysyndeton—adding the extra conjunction, *and*, instead of using a comma—"slender and silken and thrilling." The irony of the sentence is increased by the ambiguity of the word *touched*. It can be interpreted in more than one way—literally and metaphorically—disrupting the overused idiom "to be touched," meaning to be emotionally moved by someone or something. Because the sentence disrupts the cliché by playing on our senses, it sends a little thrill down our spines. Gordon's quotation demonstrates how writers can effectively break the rules—if they know what rule they are breaking.

Mixed metaphor

A poorly mixed metaphor boggles the mind and leaves the reader confused. Like using clichés, mixing your metaphors reveals lazy writing habits. You make this error when you wed two conflicting or incompatible metaphors:

> There's more than one way to skin a cat with nine lives.

There are two ways to avoid the error: 1) by using compatible vehicles for the same tenor that have the same intent, purpose, and effect or 2) by using multiple metaphors in the same sentence or passage but keeping each tenor and vessel discrete from the others. This is not as difficult as it sounds. As we saw in the review section for Part I (79), Fuentes's quotation is an excellent example of using multiple metaphors in the same passage without "mixing" them. The first half of the sentence uses a metaphor of invasion—wreaking vengeance, wilder, invading the territory—while the second half uses a metaphor of a flood—flowing, damned up, drowning, depositing. Fuentes does not err by mixing his metaphors because the first metaphor modifies the "black Irishman," while the second modifies his "dark languages."

Analogy

There are a number of definitions for analogy. However, for our purposes, an analogy is a large and complex comparison; it compares a tenor (x) to a vehicle (y), arguing that x is like y in most of its parts. For example, we can argue that a theory is analogous to a building: it has a foundation and a framework; it can be stalwart or shaky; if we haven't constructed it soundly, we might have to later buttress it with solid facts; and so on.

Analogies are often used in argument to explain an unfamiliar or questionable tenor (*x*) to the reader by comparing its similarities with a familiar vehicle (*y*).

Allegory

Allegory usually, but not always, encompasses a whole text—as in *Animal Farm*, where George Orwell creates an implied comparison between the animal farm and Communism. In other words, there is a literal level of meaning (the animal farm) and a symbolic level of meaning (Communism). Most often in allegory there is no mention of the figurative or symbolic meaning; you are simply given the literal meaning (the animal farm) and expected to not only draw the comparison yourself, but to recognize it in the first place.

John Bunyan's *Pilgrim's Progress* is an *explicit* allegorical text, and we could argue that so is Norton Juster's *Phantom Tollbooth*. In both, the main character wanders through places meeting characters with names that give away the allegory; in Bunyan's Christian tale, place names include the Celestial City and Vanity Fair where we meet characters that include Giant Despair and Hopeful. In Juster's comic tale, Milo, a chronically bored young boy, walks through a magic tollbooth into the Kingdom of Wisdom where all English idioms are taken literally, so that he finds himself jumping to (the Island of) Conclusions when he least expects it, and having adventures in the Mountains of Ignorance and the Castle in the Air. What Juster's allegory represents is not quite as exalted as Bunyan's, but perhaps it too is about salvation—only this time from boredom and indifference.

Of course, allegory is not only used as a backdrop to an entire text. In *The Republic*, Plato creates a very powerful allegory of the cave. Allegory is also used in other arts such as painting, as in the allegories of Botticelli.

Symbolism

A symbol is an image or object that represents something beyond itself. Symbols can be "public" or "private." Public symbols are those we share in a culture, such as symbols of state (the Crown) or Christianity (the Cross) or those found in advertising (Nike's swoosh). A private symbol takes its meaning from a specific context. As the writer Douglas Glover has stated, a private symbol is "an image loaded with meaning." For example, in Margaret Laurence's short story "The Loons," the title creatures symbolize the Métis people and their plight, or in another example from F. Scott Fitzgerald's novel *The Great Gatsby*, Gatsby's wealth of shirts symbolize his extravagantly mistaken beliefs. Private symbols are created when a writer loads an image with meaning by repeating it in a particular series of contexts so the reader sees the juxtaposition and makes the connection.

Personification

Personification, related to metaphor, endows human attributes to inanimate objects or abstract concepts.

> "Destiny is what you are supposed to do in life. Fate is what kicks you in the ass to make you do it." (Henry Miller)

> "When Life does not find a singer to sing her heart, she produces a philosopher to speak her mind." (Kahlil Gibran, *Sand and Foam*)

Parts of the Sentence:

Subject + Predicate
↓
Verb + Sentence Completion
↓
Objects or Complements
↓   ↓
Direct or Indirect Subject or Object

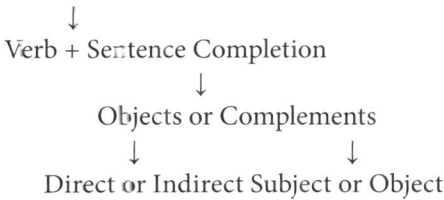

Subject

The subject of a sentence is what or who is doing the action or experiencing the state of being of the finite verb. The subject can be a concrete or abstract noun, pronoun, infinitive, infinite phrase, gerund, gerund phrase, or noun clause.

A subject may be simple or compound.

- **Simple subject:** A *simple* subject is not necessarily a word in its singular form; *simple* refers to the subject as a single unit (*many people, my sore throats*):

  > "*Many people* lose their tempers merely from seeing you keep yours." (F.M. Colby)

- **Compound subject:** A *compound* subject is made up of two or more subjects, all connected to the finite verb and joined by a coordinating conjunction:

  > "*Timing, degree, and conviction* are the three wise men in this life." (R. I. Fitzhenry)

Subjects can also be more complex, as in the following example of a *complete subject* from Max Beerbohm's comic novel *Zuleika Dobson*:

> "*The fading signals and grey eternal walls of that antique station, which, familiar to them and insignificant, does yet whisper to the tourist the last enchantments of the Middle Age.*"

The subject answers a question: *what?* or *who? What* whispers to the tourist? *That* whispers to the tourist, meaning, *the fading signals and grey eternal walls of that antique station, familiar and insignificant to them.* In this example of a *complete subject*, the essence of the subject is *signals and walls.* The clause in which the verb is omitted—*which (are) familiar to them and insignificant*—modifies the compound subject (*signals and walls*), as does the prepositional phrase, *of that antique station.*

Although the rhythm of Beerbohm's sentence is truly eloquent, because language evolves, we might write this sentence a little differently today. We would still use the complex subject, but our language is slightly more concise:

> The fading signals and grey eternal walls of that antique station, although familiar and insignificant to them, still whisper to the tourist the last enchantments of the Middle Age.

Predicate

The predicate of a sentence consists of the finite verb and sentence completion. A finite verb, you will remember, is a verb that inflects (changes its endings).

The finite verb is also known as the simple predicate or main verb. A finite verb may be simple or compound. When simple, the verb is the same as the simple predicate or finite verb. When compound, two or more verbs are connected to the same subject, joined by a conjunction.

For review, find the simple and compound verbs, plus the verbals, in this opening paragraph from *The English Patient* by Michael Ondaatje:

> She stands up in the garden where she has been working and looks into the distance. She has sensed a shift in the weather. There is another gust of wind, a buckle of noise in the air, and the tall cypresses sway. She turns and moves uphill towards the house, climbing over a low wall, feeling the first drops of rain on her bare arms. She crosses the loggia and quickly enters the house.

- *stands up and looks* is a compound verb of the subject *she.*
- *where she has been working* is a clause with a simple verb (*has been working*) connected to its subject (*she*)—this clause interrupts the main clause.
- *she has sensed a shift in the weather* is a simple sentence consisting of a subject (*she*) and a simple verb (*has sensed*).
- *there is another gust of wind,* [*there is*] *a buckle of noise in the air, and the tall cypresses sway*—Here we have three independent clauses (a triad) joined by a coordinating conjunction (*and*), each with a simple verb (*is, is* [ellipsis], *sway*). (This is one way of interpreting the ellipsis.)
- *turns and moves* is another compound verb joined by and.
- *climbing over a low wall, feeling the first drops of rain on her bare arms* is made up of two participial phrases (verbals).

- *she crosses the loggia and quickly enters the house* also consists of a compound verb (*crosses and enters*) and a subject (*she*).

Objects and complements

Objects and/or complements are components of the sentence completion. Here is where our analysis of the sentence becomes a little more complex. But stay with me, it gets easier.

As a side note, you should know that sentence completions are sometimes referred to as complements. Now that you know this, set it aside. It is less confusing if you think of the broader category as sentence completions and the limited category as complements.

As we have discussed, all predicates are made up of the finite verb and sentence completion. We then break down sentence completion into two categories: objects and complements. The difference is not always obvious, at first. Think of objects as something (concrete or abstract) distinctly separate from the subject, whereas complements describe, modify, or in some way enhance the subject (or object).

Objects receive the action of the transitive verb. They are direct or indirect. The indirect object can precede the direct object:

<blockquote>
s.   v.   ind. obj.   dir. obj.
They offered *the winner* a choice. (They offered *what*? A choice—
the object.)
</blockquote>

The indirect object can also follow the direct object:

<blockquote>
s.   v.   dir. obj.   ind. obj.
They offered a choice to *the winner.*
</blockquote>

When it follows the object, the indirect object appears in a phrase.

Complements describe or modify. There are two types: subject complements and object complements. *Subject complements* describe or modify the subject of a sentence. They include predicate nouns and predicate adjectives.

<blockquote>
s. v.   subject complement
Plato is *a political philosopher.* (predicate noun)
</blockquote>

<blockquote>
s. (gerund) v.   subject complement
Reading Plato is *enlightening.* (predicate adjective)
</blockquote>

Object complements describe or modify objects:

<blockquote>
s.   v.   indirect obj.   obj.   obj. complement
They offered the winner a choice *of options.*
</blockquote>

Note how *of options* describes the object, *choice.*

Parts of Speech

Nouns

A noun is a person, place, thing, or idea. It can be concrete or abstract, proper or common, mass or count:

- Concrete nouns are tangible; they exist as objects in the world or universe: *table, tree, planets*. Abstract nouns are intangible: *love, biology, silence, justice*.
- Proper nouns name a specific person, place, or thing and are capitalized: *Barack Obama, Prague, Mona Lisa*. Common nouns name all others and are not capitalized.
- Mass nouns refer to something that cannot be counted; they do not inflect: *gold* (no matter how much or how little remains, it is still called *gold*); the same holds true for pasta, oxygen, and abstract nouns such as happiness and justice. Count nouns do inflect—they usually take *-s* or *-es* to show more than one: *word/words, fox/foxes*.

To show possession, nouns inflect by adding an apostrophe + *s*: *Karsh's photograph, the essay's conclusion*. Or in the case of a word already ending in *-s*, they take only an apostrophe: *the writers' union*.

Pronouns

A pronoun takes the place of a noun (its antecedent or referent). A pronoun must have an antecedent that is not too far off. The antecedent should precede the pronoun whenever possible. If you use more than one pronoun in a sentence, make sure the antecedents are clear.

There are eight types of pronouns:

- Personal pronouns (e.g. *he, she, it*) take the place of nouns.

  When Saunders *entered* the race, did *he* remember to wear *his* number?

- Interrogative pronouns (e.g. *how, what, which, who, whose*) construct questions.

  Who was the grand-prize winner?

- Indefinite pronouns (e.g. *everyone, both, some, few, something*) do not refer to any particular antecedent.

  Something should be done about the error. *Few* noticed.

  These are exceptions to the basic pronoun rules and should be used cautiously because they can cause vagueness and ambiguity in your writing.

- Relative pronouns (e.g. *that, which, what*) refer to their antecedents and link them to a clause. These are also referred to as "functional relatives."

  In case of a tie, *which* is very unlikely, they will split the prize.

- Demonstrative pronouns (e.g. *this, that, these, those*) point to something.

  That contestant is cheating. *Those* are not acceptable shoes.

- Reciprocal pronouns (e.g. *each other, one another*) form reciprocal relationships.

  They eyed *one another.*

- Reflexive pronouns (e.g. *myself, yourself, itself, ourselves*) are used only when the subject and the object are the same.

  She disappointed *herself.*

  He seemed uncomfortable with *himself.*

- Intensive pronouns are similar to reflexive pronouns, but they are used as appositives for emphasis.

  I, *myself*, doubted his word.

- Expletive pronouns (e.g. *it, this, there*) act as subjects but do not refer to any particular antecedent.

  It is a good idea to avoid expletives whenever possible.

  By nature, expletives are vague, but especially so when you use them to refer to compound or complex ideas or whole previous paragraphs, as in *this proves that* . . . . Expletives are not effective in this descriptive role. In fact, it is always a good idea to see if you can replace an expletive with a precise word—what you actually mean—you won't always be able to, but you will be surprised how often substituting the precise word is effective, and how much clearer your writing will become when you do.

Case
There are three cases of pronouns:

- nominative case or subject form (*I, you, he, she, it, we, they*).
- objective case or object form (*me, you, him, her, it, us, them*).
- possessive case, which has a subject and object form (*my/mine, your/yours, his, her/hers, its, our/ours, their/theirs*).

If you look up the word *my* in the dictionary, it is described as an (attributive) adjective. This is somewhat confusing because *my* is a pronoun in the possessive case used to modify a noun (*my life, my desires, a room of my own*), which is the role of an adjective. This is precisely what drives students of English mad. . . .

If you find yourself being driven mad by the choice between *I* and *me*, what you need to know is that *I* is the subject; *me* is the object:

I want to dance the night away. (*I* is the subject.)

He wants to dance with me. (*Me* is the object.)

Josh and me/I will dance tonight. (Which should you use here? Hint: ignore *Josh* and the choice is obvious.)

Will he want to dance with me/I? (Hint: does the sentence end with a subject or an object?)

The subject/object distinction also helps you to choose between *like* and *as*. *As* is a conjunction; *like* is a preposition (similes are prepositional phrases). Prepositions, you'll remember, take objects:

My best friend thinks like me.

My best friend thinks as I (do).

The choice that throws us the most is when the pronoun comes at the end of a sentence that already has a subject, and it still takes the subjective form of the pronoun. I like to think of these constructions as eclipsed clauses:

She is better looking than I (am).

He knows the winner is I. (He knows that I am the winner.)

However, the choice can be a little more difficult. Predicate pronouns acting as subjective complements are not always easy to discern at first:

Who is your leader? I am she.

In this example, *she* is the complement to *I*. A subjective complement identifies or explains the subject (the antecedent to *she* is *I, the leader*). The clue is the linking verb—remember that although linking verbs are transitive (they need something to complete them), they do not take objects. They are completed by complements that further describe or explain or identify.

If all that sounds like Greek to you, there is a rule of thumb that makes the choice easier: *Any form of the verb "to be" used as a finite verb must be preceded and followed by the same case.* Translated, this means that if you use a subject case on one side of the finite verb *be* (*am, is, was, were, will be*, etc.), you *must* use the subject case on the other side:

It was I.

Do you think it might have been she?

I am she.

You can see that this language is in a state of evolution. How many English speakers still follow this rule? Before long, this rule could completely disappear. Of course, you can always ignore the problem by answering: I *am*. But Flaubert might call that a sleight of hand!

Adjectives and articles

An adjective modifies (describes or limits) a noun or pronoun. Adjectives that limit are categorized further as demonstrative (*this, those, that*); interrogative (*whose, what*); indefinite (*either, any, some*), numerical (*seven, first, fifth*); possessive (*my, mine, your, his, our*); and articles (*the, a, an*).

An adjective can take one of two positions: 1) preceding the noun it modifies (*a complicated reason*) and 2) following the verb in the predicate (*the reason was complicated*), where it is known as a predicate adjective. The indefinite articles *a* and *an* and the definite article *the* always precede the noun.

One common difficulty that students encounter is deciding when to use an adverb and when to use a predicate adjective. Here's a helpful rule: use a predicate adjective after verbs of the five senses (*look, sound, smell, taste,* and *feel*) unless they mean action, in which case use an adverb.

The blanket is soft.
The blanket feels soft.
Adverb: The blanket fell softly to the floor.

The noise is harsh.
The noise sounds harsh.
Adverb: The noise echoed harshly across the room.

The apple is bad.
The apple tasted bad.
Adverb: He behaved badly.

Adverbs

An adverb modifies a verb, adjective, or other adverb. It usually tells one of three things: how, when, or where.

It can take one of two positions: 1) before a verb (*she gently tore the bandage away from the wound*), adjective (*The incision was extremely deep*), or other adverb (*she applied the medication very quickly*) and 2) immediately following a verb (*she spoke softly into his ear*).

You may have noticed that many, but not all, adverbs end with *-ly*. Speaking etymologically, *-ly* originally designated *like*, so *softly* meant "softlike" and *hardly* meant "hardlike."

Verbs

Verbs describe actions or states. There are four principal forms of a verb, whether the verb is regular or irregular: infinitive (*to walk, to fall, to be*); past tense (*walked, fell, was/were*); past participle (*walked, fallen, been*); and present participle (*walking, falling, being*). These four basic forms can be used to create all other forms of a verb.

With the help of auxiliary verbs, we can modify these principal forms to indicate a subtle range of meaning. These modal (mood creating) auxiliary verbs include *can, could, may, might, must, could, should,* and *would*.

Verbs are the most highly inflected part of speech. You can express a wide palette of meaning by changing the ending or inflecting a verb's person (first, second, third), number (singular or plural), tense (past, present, future, etc.), aspect (progressive, emphatic, inchoative, repetitive), mood (indicative, imperative, interrogative, subjunctive), and voice (active, passive).

Person and number

A verb is inflected in person and number according to its subject. When the subject is *I* (singular) or *we* (plural), the verb appears in the first person: *I like/ we like, I am/we are*. When the subject is *you* (singular and plural), the verb appears in the second person: *you like; you are*. When the subject is *he, she,* or *it* (singular) or *they* (plural), the verb appears in the third person: *he/she/it likes, they like, he/she/it is, they are*.

Tense

Verb tense refers to the form the verb takes to indicate the time of the action (past, present, or future) or its completeness (perfect tense). So, think of *tense* as *time*; perfect, in this context, means completed time.

Consider the following examples:

She will dance at the Jubilee Auditorium.

Next week, *she will have danced* at the Jubilee Auditorium.

The first example is in the third-person *future tense*, which identifies that the action will occur in the future. The second example is in the third-person *future perfect tense*, which expresses an expected completion of the action at some future point in time.

An English speaker is familiar with these tenses, but not always with their labels:

Tense	Simple	Perfect
Present	I dance.	I have danced.
Past	I danced.	I had danced.
Future	I will dance.	I will have danced.

For practice, identify the verb tenses in the following quotation:

> It has usually seemed self evident to people that such things as trees and mountains and animals belong in one domain, and such things as houses and laws and dictionaries belong to another. We have often distinguished between "nature" and "civilization," the naturally given and the man-made. And the distinction has played a part in the kinds of order we see and make in the world.
>
> This rough-and-ready division has survived dramatic changes in cosmology, which have sometimes altered the actual meanings of "nature" and "civilization" out of all recognition. A tree, for instance, has one cluster of meanings when located in the cosmos revealed by medieval Christian faith, and a largely different cluster of meanings in the cosmos revealed by the physical sciences. One cannot speak of the concepts "nature" and "civilization" as though they had meant the same things throughout history, then. But the distinction itself has nonetheless been an enduring one. (Dennis Lee, *Savage Fields*)

Aspect

There is one more form of the verb that we must take into consideration: the aspect of continuance—an ongoing or continuing action. Because this factor refers more to an event than to time itself, we call this an *aspect*, rather than a *tense*. Consider the following example:

> When J.F. Kennedy died, she was storming Parliament Hill.

The progressive aspect refers to the event of Kennedy's death: she was doing this *when* Kennedy was shot.

The progressive aspect combines with tense to give an accurate description of what is happening in a sentence. The *present progressive* aspect describes something that is ongoing or continuing in the present. The *past progressive* aspect describes something ongoing in the past, before something else happened. The *future progressive* aspect describes something ongoing in the future.

Now we can add aspect to our tense chart:

Tense	Simple	Perfect	Progressive	Perfect Progressive
Present	I dance.	I have danced.	I am dancing.	I have been dancing.
Past	I danced.	I had danced.	I was dancing.	I had been dancing.
Future	I will dance.	I will have danced.	I will be dancing.	I will have been dancing.

Mood

There are four moods of the verb:

- indicative—used to express a statement,
- interrogative—used to express a question,
- imperative—used to express a command, and
- subjunctive—used to express a wish, doubt, or condition.

We examined mood in depth in lesson 6, but, here, I would like to revisit the subjunctive mood. A verb in the *subjunctive mood* expresses a wish, regret, request, doubt, proposal, or condition. The following are verbs often followed by clauses that take the subjunctive: *ask, move, order, pray, prefer, recommend, regret, request, require, suggest,* and *wish.*

The subjunctive form takes the third-person singular present tense and the verb *to be.* Regardless of what the subject is, the subjunctive mood of the verb *to be* is *be* in the present tense and *were* in the past tense. In other words: in the present tense, use *be* for all persons; in the past tense, use *were* for all persons, including the first person: *I wish I <u>were</u> computer literate.*

In modern usage, the subjunctive is usually found in subordinate clauses, as in the following examples:

> The prerequisite is that everyone *be* computer literate. (The subordinate clause follows the main clause with a demand.)

> If I *were* you, I would take the course. (The verb follows *if* and expresses a non-factual condition.)

> I just wish I *were* able to type faster. (The second verb is in a clause following a verb expressing a wish.)

> She recommends that each student *report* his or her level of ability. (In regular verbs, the third-person singular present tense in the subjunctive mood drops the *-s* or *-es.*)

Somerset Maugham, *Fowler's Modern English Usage,* and more recent grammar texts all suggest that the subjunctive mood is dying (if not dead). Fowler has a useful distinction between what he calls four categories of present usage: alives, revivals, survivals, and arrivals. "Alives" are subjunctive constructs that are still in use in our natural form of speech. For everyday folks like you and me, Fowler would like to restrict usage to the "alives" because he finds that, to most people, the grammar of the subjunctive is "not natural but artificial," which causes people to make errors, even if they know better. "Alives" include:

- second-person imperatives: *Go away.*
- third-person imprecations: *Manners be hanged!*
- idioms: *Come what may . . . . Be that as it may . . . . Far be it from me . . . .*

- clauses that express a hypothesis that is not a fact: *I wish it were over* . . . . *If he were here now* . . . .
- *though, . . . be phrases: Though all care be exercised* . . .
- formal motions: *I move that Mr. Smith be appointed* . . . .

The following passage, taken from J.W. Gregory's *The Making of the Earth*, demonstrates how the subjunctive mood was formerly used. Gregory illustrates the movement of the members of the solar system—that is, on a single plane and moving in the same direction—by an analogy of a mop:

When the mop is at rest its head is nearly spherical. If it be spun swiftly the shape becomes flattened like a disc thick in the middle and thinner towards the edge, and the water in the mop is thrown off as drops which keep in the plane of the flattened mop head. If the mop be wet with greasy water and it be spun horizontally over a smooth surface then the drops thrown off may be seen to fly outward and also to move forward in the same direction as the movement of the mop, and each drop will spin in the same direction. Similarly if the major and minor planets and planet-esimals were all formed from a vast loose body which was spinning around its centre, they should all move forward in the same direction, and unless disturbed by later influences should all revolve in the same direction.

This passage was written in 1912. How would we write it today?

Voice
In the active voice, the subject performs the action:

I wrote this essay.

In the passive voice, the subject is acted upon:

This essay was written by me. (We can recognize the passive voice by the added auxiliary verb *to be*: was *written*.)

In general, try to use the active voice whenever possible. It is more concise, more direct, and more dynamic. However, do not ignore the passive voice altogether—it has its place. For example, the passive voice can draw the reader's attention to the object when the subject is less significant (*thirteen people were killed in the avalanche*) or to deflect blame for the action from the subject (*the salary cuts were implemented by the general manager*).

Finite verbs
Finite verbs are the main verbs of a sentence—the verb needed to make the subject/verb connection of a complete thought in a clause or a sentence. They must agree with the subject in person and number. The finite verb is what the subject is doing or experiencing, or the state it is in. As discussed above, finite

verbs inflect—their endings change to indicate number, person, tense, aspect, mood, and voice.

Finite verbs are *transitive, intransitive,* or *linking:*

- A transitive verb requires an object to complete it:

  She tossed the pancakes. She stated her position.

- An intransitive verb does not require an object to complete its meaning:

  He argued. He agreed.

- Note: some verbs can be transitive or intransitive depending on the context:

  I believe you.

  I believe.

- A linking verb is transitive in the sense that it needs something to complete it, but not an object. We call its completion *a complement.* Complements identify, describe, or explain subjects or verbs. The most common linking verb is *is.*

  s.   apposition   v. subject complement
Joyce's last novel, <u>Finnegan's Wake</u>, *is dense and difficult.*

The complement (*dense and difficult*) describes the subject (*Joyce's last novel*). The appositive is non-restrictive because *last novel* already specifies which of Joyce's novels is dense and difficult.

Linking verbs also include verbs of the five senses: *see, taste, feel, smell,* and *touch.*

s. v.   verb complement
Joyce felt *alienated by his uncomprehending audience.*

The verb complement describes the linking verb (*felt*).

Non-finite verbs (verbals)
Non-finite verbs (or verbals) do not have to agree with the subject, so they do not inflect; they always remain in the same form. You cannot substitute a non-finite verb for a finite verb.

There are three forms of non-finite verbs:

- infinitive—a verb in its infinitive (or dictionary) form: *to be, to write, to fly:*

  I desire *to write,* or *to hang glide,* or somehow *to express* my existence.

- gerund—a verb acting as a noun; gerunds use the -*ing* form:

  In our time, *flying* has become *dangerous*.

- Sometimes gerunds combine with infinitive verbs to form the subject:

  Learning to fly a plane takes time and *money*.

- participle—a verb in the present or past participle form (the present form uses -*ing*, as in *walking*; the past form uses -*ed*, as in *walked*):

  I studied, *learning* to fly on the wings of thought, *throttling* the engine of my passion.

Prepositions

Prepositions show relationship. Imagine holding a basketball in front of a hoop. The ball may go *in* the net, *to* the net, *through* the net, *over*, *under*, *beside*, *around*, or *behind* the net, and so on. These words show the relationship between the ball and the hoop. They are prepositions.

Because prepositions show relationship, they *must* take an object (*she went down the road*, *behind the desk*, *over the bridge*; *he was within his right*). You may pile them up, as James Joyce does in the following quotation, but eventually they must take an object:

"The artist, like the God of the creation, remains within or behind or beyond or above his handiwork, invisible, refined out of existence, indifferent, paring his fingernails." (*A Portrait of the Artist as a Young Man*)

In this example, the finite verb is *remains*; the object of the prepositions is *his handiwork*.

Prepositions can be compounds made up of two or more words: *with regard to*, *aside from*, *in addition to*, *in case of*.

Conjunctions

Conjunctions are linking words. There are two types: coordinating and subordinating. Coordinating conjunctions include correlative conjunctions and conjunctive adverbs, also discussed below.

Coordinating conjunctions link words, phrases, and clauses of equal weight and significance, and of similar form and function. Each coordinating conjunction indicates a specific relationship: *and* (addition), *but* (contrast), *for* (reason, cause), *or* (choice), *nor* (negative addition), *so* (effect, result), and *yet* (opposition).

In the following passage, examine how author Enos Mills, when describing an avalanche, has used coordinating conjunctions to join words, phrases, and clauses:

There was no time to bid farewell to fears when the slide started, *nor* to enter-tain them while running away from it. Instinct put me to flight; the situation set my wits working at their best, *and*, once started, I could neither stop *nor* look back; *and* so thick *and* fast did obstructions *and* dangers rise before me that only dimly *and* incidentally did I think of the oncoming danger behind. (*The Spell of the Rockies*)

The first *nor* joins two phrases: *to bid farewell to fears when the slide started* and *to entertain them while running away from it.* The second *nor* links the words *stop* and *look back.* The first two *ands* link clauses: *the situation set my wits working at their best*; *I could neither stop nor look back*; and *so thick and fast . . . oncoming danger behind.* The final three *ands* link words: *thick* and *fast*; *obstructions* and *dangers*; *dimly* and *incidentally.*

Correlative conjunctions also link units of equal significance. This type of conjunction includes the following pairs of words: *neither/nor, but/and, either/ or, not/but,* and *not only/but also.* These pairs join two grammatical units with the same form and function.

To recognize correlative conjunctions, remember that the second word of the pair must be a coordinating conjunction. Correlative conjunctions form a set within the larger category of "correlatives," which are pairs of words used together to indicate a mutual or corresponding relationship (*if/then*).

Conjunctive adverbs join independent clauses. They include the following terms: *additionally, also, besides, consequently, for example, furthermore, in addition, moreover, nevertheless, otherwise, similarly, still, then, therefore,* and *thus.* They are preceded by a semicolon and followed by a comma:

I read it; *however,* I still do not understand it.

When choosing which conjunctive adverb to use, it is crucial to think of the role each one plays; that is, the relationship it expresses. Do you need to express the relationship of time (*at the same time, earlier*), logic (*however, as a result, therefore*), comparison (*similarly, likewise*), consequence (*as a result, accordingly*), contrast (*on the contrary, conversely*), or contradiction (*nonethe-less, yet*)? Do you want to sum up, digress, specify, or express uncertainty (*per-haps, possibly*)? Using the correct conjunctive adverb will always improve your argument. These adverbs help the reader follow your train of thought.

Subordinating conjunctions begin dependent clauses and subordinate them to the main clause, forming complex sentences; that is, sentences con-sisting of at least one independent (main) clause and one dependent (sub-ordinate) clause. They include the following words: *although, as, because, even though, however, if, since, that, until, whereas, whether, which, what, why,* and *who.*

For an example, let's return to Mills's avalanche:

The slide did not slow down, and so closely did it crowd me *that*, through the crashing of trees *as* it struck them down, I could hear the rocks and splintered timbers in its mass grinding together and thudding against obstructions over *which* it swept. These sounds and broken, flying limbs cried to me "Faster!" and as I started to descend another steep moraine, I threw away my staff and "let go."

Polysyndeton and asyndeton

Polysyndeton and asyndeton are constructions involving conjunctions. They can help create variation, rhythm, and mood.

Polysyndeton is the addition of conjunctions. Most often, a writer will add an extra *and* in a series, as Joan Didion does in the following excerpt from her story "Some Dreamers of the Golden Dream," *Slouching Towards Bethlehem* setting the stage for murder:

"There has been no rain since April. Every voice seems a scream. It is the season of suicide *and* divorce and prickly dread, wherever the wind blows."

Asyndeton is the omission of conjunctions. Most often, a writer will omit the final *and* in a series:

"January 11, 1965, was a bright warm day in southern California, the kind of day when Catalina floats on the Pacific horizon and the air smells of orange blossoms and it is a long way from the bleak and difficult East, a long way from the cold, a long way from the past." (Joan Didion, "Some Dreamers of the Golden Dream," *Slouching Towards Bethlehem*)

Interjections

The final part of speech, which is not always included in the list, is interjection. In writing, interjections usually take the form of one or two words used in front of a sentence, detached from the rest of the meaning by an end stop and simply expressing an emotion (*Hurray! Oh! Indeed. Oh well.*), as in the movie *My Fair Lady* when Henry Higgins mutters:

"*Damn! Damn! Damn! Damn!* I've grown accustomed to her face." (Alan Lerner)

However, in speech and dialogue, interjections sometimes fall in the middle of a sentence. In fact, the word *interjection* comes from Latin (*inter* meaning "between" and *iacere* meaning "throw"), meaning "thrown in between":

"It is useful to see, in the Frankfurtean integration of the Marxist and post-Freudian schools, a focus on the ways in which culture (in late-capitalist, capitalist and, *indeed*, prior economic forms) serves the exploitation, the undoing of our human potential." (Greg Pyrcz. *Political Studies: A Survey of Core Approaches*)

Phrases

A phrase is a group of words, without a subject/verb connection, acting as a part of speech. Phrases may act as adjectives or adverbs or nouns. There are four main types of phrases: prepositional, participle, infinitive, and gerund.

Prepositional phrase

Prepositional phrases begin with a preposition and always take objects: *into the dark, without exception, in summary*. They act as adjectives, adverbs, or, occasionally, nouns. The following quotation contains two prepositional phrases:

> "*In the country of the blind* the one eyed-man is king." (Desiderius Erasmus, *Adagia*)

Participial phrase

Participial phrases (usually) begin with a participle and may be formed with either the present or past participle. They act as adjectives:

> "History is philosophy *learned from examples*." (Dionysius of Halicarnassus)

> "Core approaches in critical studies make different assumptions about the source of our conduct, *adopting different folk theories of human agency*; but all hold to the view that inherent to our everyday lives are processes of repression, the denial of the natural, potential and emergent features of our humanity." (Greg Pyrcz, *Political Studies*)

In the first example, the participial phrase begins with a past participle; in the second example, it begins with a present participle.

Infinitive phrase

Infinitive phrases (usually) begin with an infinitive. They act as adjectives, adverbs, or nouns. The following quotation contains an exception—an infinitive noun-phrase acting as the subject, but not starting with the infinitive:

> "*Thoroughly to teach another* is the best way to learn for yourself."
> (Tryon Edwards, *A Dictionary of Thoughts*)

Although using the emphatic device of inversion throws emphasis on *thoroughly*, we would probably not use Edwards's construction (starting with the adverb) today, as it sounds stilted. Another translation states: "If you would know anything thoroughly, teach it to others."

Gerundive phrase

Gerundive (or gerundial) phrases begin with a gerund. They always function as a noun, acting as a subject, complement, or object of the preposition:

Smoking in bed is a dying habit. (Here, the gerundive phrase functions as the subject.)

"Aggression is *showing people* you are out of control." (Here, the gerundive phrase functions as the subject complement.) (Lynne Brennan)

Both the gerundive phrase and present participle phrase begin with an -*ing* word. However, a gerundive phase functions as a noun, whereas a present participle phrase functions as an adjective.

Tip: You should be able to substitute the gerund phrase with the word "this."

Absolute phrase

Absolutes are constructs within a sentence that are only loosely tied to the main idea, modifying the whole idea of the main clause rather than a particular grammatical unit. An absolute phrase is often, but not always, found at the beginning of a sentence:

"*From error to error* one discovers the entire truth." (Sigmund Freud, *The Interpretation of Dreams*)

"The butler entered the room, *a solemn procession of one*." (P.G. Wodehouse)

To review, identify the phrases in the following quotation by Hannah Arendt:

"In order to go on living one must try to escape the death involved in perfectionism." (*Rahel Varnhagen: The Life of a Jewess*)

Tip: Identify the finite verb first. Where is the subject/verb connection?

Punctuation

We think of the rules of punctuation as being written in stone, but, in fact, the conventions of punctuation evolve with the language. And the experienced writer has the choice to follow a convention, or not. The role of punctuation is to ease the burden of the reader. The conventions of punctuation help not only to clarify, but also to predict what is coming—an essential skill in reading. These functions are effective only if we agree to use punctuation marks in the same way, consistently. Take the following sentence: *The hungry guns kill.* We can change the meaning drastically simply by adding a comma: *The hungry, guns kill.* In the first example, *hungry* is an adjective in a simple sentence; in the second example, *hungry* is a noun in an inverted sentence. The punctuation mark changes the meaning of the utterance.

However, punctuation also performs other important functions—such as setting rhythm or providing emphasis—which may persuade a writer, occasionally, to ignore a particular convention. The punctuation marks that are the most flexible in this regard are those that occur most commonly within a sentence: the comma, colon, semicolon, and dash.

Period, question mark, and exclamation point

The most straightforward rules govern the use of end punctuation, and students rarely mix up these punctuation marks. The period is used to end declarative and imperative sentences, as well as to end abbreviations (*Dr.*, *St.*). The exclamation point is used at the end of an exclamatory sentence; the question mark is used at the end of a question.

Comma

A comma can be used to separate a list of words, or a series of phrases or clauses:

> "Being unable to remove the chain, I jumped over, and, running up the flagged causeway bordered with straggling gooseberry bushes, knocked vainly for admittance, till my knuckles tingled and the dogs howled." (Emily Brontë, *Wuthering Heights*)

The commas here indicate non-restrictive clauses and participial phrases. They help the reader follow the action. Brontë has very carefully constructed the sequence of events in a logical order so as not to lose her reader—the punctuation accentuates this order. It would not be effective to break the convention in this case.

Commas separate independent clauses joined with a coordinating conjunction; whereas, parataxis (a semicolon) joins independent clauses with no conjunction. See if you can explain the use of commas and semicolons in the following quotation:

> "I expect to pass through this world but once; any good thing therefore that I can do, or any kindness that I can show to any fellow-creature, let me do it now; let me not defer or neglect it, for I shall not pass this way again." (Stephen Grellet)

To understand Grellet's use of punctuation, identify the clauses, both restrictive and non-restrictive. A slight rewriting may help:

> I expect to pass through this world but once; therefore, any good thing that I can do, or any kindness that I can show to any fellow-creature, let me do it now; let me not defer or neglect it, for I shall not pass this way again.

- *I expect to pass through this world but once* (independent clause)
- *therefore, any good thing* (conjunctive adverb beginning a clause, in its simplest form—*let me do any good thing or kindness now*—but in the present form it begins a coordinated phrase that acts as antecedent—*any good thing and any kindness*—to *it*)
- *that I can do* (restrictive clause modifying *thing*, no commas)

- *or any kindness* (coordinating conjunction joining coordinated phrases)
- *that I can show to my fellow-creature* (restrictive clause modifying *kindness*, no commas)
- *let me do it now* (independent clause—imperative)
- *let me not defer or neglect* (independent clause—imperative)
- *for I shall not pass this way again* (coordinating conjunction joining independent clauses).

A comma can also be used to separate a word, phrase, or clause introducing the main clause:

Unable to remove the chain, I jumped over the wall.

A comma can separate an absolute from the rest of the sentence:

"I am about to take my last voyage, *a great leap in the dark*." (the last words of Thomas Hobbes)

Similarly, a comma can separate an appositive:

"The village of Holcomb stands on the high wheat plains of western Kansas, *a lonesome area that other Kansans call 'out there'*." (Truman Capote, *In Cold Blood*)

"My father, *a fat, funny man with beautiful eyes and a subversive wit*, is trying to decide which of his eight children he will take with him to the county fair." (Alice Walker, *In Search of Our Mothers' Gardens*)

But remember that appositives can also be separated by dashes:

"The authentic and pure values—*truth, beauty, and goodness*—in the activity of the human being are the result of one and the same act, a certain application of the full attention to the object." (Simone Weil, *Gravity and Grace*)

Or parenthesis:

"Although the students and amateurs of culture in the non Arab Muslim world (*all of what was once known as Persia, and the Sikh and Moghul territories of northern India*) have long known something about its poetry and poetic traditions, these alien poetics have, until recently, had little impact on the English-speaking world." (Douglas Barbour, *Beyond Tish*)

Finally, commas separate interruptions and inversions:

"But here, *unless I am mistaken*, is our client." (Sir Arthur Conan Doyle, *The Adventure of Wisteria Lodge*)

The conventions most often broken by writers involve the use of the comma. But remember, a good writer always knows the convention she or he is breaking. There are two rules that are (almost) never broken:

- Do not use commas with restrictive phrases or clauses.
- Do not use commas to separate the main elements of a sentence; that is, do not use a comma to separate a subject from its verb, a verb from its object, or a verb from its complement. (You will, of course, put commas around any non-restrictive interrupting words, phrases, or clauses.)

Punctuation evolves along with the other elements of language. For example, in the nineteenth century Jane Austen wrote the following:

"I have been a selfish being, all my life, in practice, though not in principle." (*Pride and Prejudice*)

Today, we would be more likely to write this as follows:

I have been a selfish being all my life, in practice, but not in principle.

Deleting the comma subdues the emphasis on *all my life* and throws it more heavily on *in practice*. The writer would be ignoring a comma convention, but knowingly, for a good reason.

Semicolon

A semicolon is used primarily in compound sentences: in parataxis, which we have discussed as one method of joining independent clauses, and before a conjunctive adverb. But it is also used to separate items in a list, when one or more of the items contains a comma:

We have studied several Canadians: Margaret Atwood, author of *Wilderness*; David Suzuki, the environmentalist; and George Elliott Clarke, the poet and dramatist.

However, writers break rules. You will come across clauses and lists where commas are required, but the writer has separated them by semicolons. Why? For emphasis. The semicolon provides a longer stop than a comma, as the colon provides a longer stop than a semicolon.

Colon

A colon is used after a formal salutation (*Dear Sir:*), between hours and minutes (*9:30*), and to announce elements such as a list, an afterthought, or an important idea:

"There are three kinds of lies: lies, damned lies, and statistics." (Benjamin Disraeli)

"Insanity: doing the same thing over and over again and expecting different results." (Albert Einstein)

"I think novelists perform many useful tasks for their fellow citizens, but one of the most valuable is this: enabling us to see ourselves as others see us." (Doris Lessing, *Prisons We Choose to Live Inside*)

Try using a colon in the following quotation by Dante Alighieri, to form one emphatic sentence. Do you need to add or invert anything else?

"Avarice, envy, pride. Three fatal sparks, have set the hearts of all on Fire." (*The Divine Comedy*)

Dash

The dash (—) is not the same as a hyphen (-), which joins some compound words. The dash has no function of its own, but sometimes replaces the comma, semicolon, colon, or parenthesis. It is more emphatic and produces a longer stop when substituted for a comma; and it is less formal when substituted for a colon or semicolon or parenthesis.

The following quotation is an example of a dash standing in for a comma:

"The authentic and pure values—*truth, beauty, and goodness*—in the activity of a human being are the result of one and the same act, a certain application of the ful attention to the object." (Simone Weil, *Gravity and Grace*)

Here, the dash replaces a semicolon:

"It's not true that life is one damn thing after another—it's one damn thing over and over." (Edna St. Vincent Millay)

"Fear succeeds crime—it is its punishment." (Voltaire)

Finally, we have an example of a dash standing in for a colon:

"It takes two to speak the truth—one to speak, and another to hear." (Henry David Thoreau)

Restrictive and Non-restrictive Elements

A restrictive element cannot be removed without changing the meaning of a sentence or clause. A restrictive word or phrase is essential to the meaning of the clause in which it is found; a restrictive (dependent) clause is essential to the meaning of the main clause. To indicate that they are essential, restrictive elements do not take commas.

Non-restrictive elements provide additional information. They can be removed without changing the meaning of a sentence or a clause. To indicate that they are not essential, they take commas.

(For examples, see **clauses** and **appositives**.)

Sentences

There are five kinds of sentences: simple, compound, complex, compound-complex, and fragment. The number and type of clauses contained within the sentence determine its classification.

Simple sentence

A simple sentence has one independent clause; it is a complete thought. Whether short or long, a simple sentence has only one subject/verb connection. You can pile up subjects or verbs, but as long as one subject is doing all the finite verbs, or all the subjects are doing the same finite verb, or all the subjects are doing all the same finite verbs, there is only one subject/verb connection. Simple sentences can be extended by the use of phrases.

The *short* simple sentence is used for clarity, variety, and emphasis:

> "Advertising is legalized lying." (H.G. Wells)

Compound sentence

A compound sentence has at least two independent clauses joined by a coordinating conjunction, parataxis, a conjunctive adverb, or correlative conjunctions. When the two independent clauses are very short, you can use a comma instead of a semicolon to join them in parataxis. The independent clauses are equal in weight and significance, and have the same form and function. The following compound sentence, written by Voltaire in the 1700s, has taken on new meaning in our time:

> "Men argue, nature acts."

Triad

A triad has three independent clauses arranged in a parallel construction. Here's an example that illustrates a triadic pattern but with more complexity than the usual triad, as each part of the triad, joined by parataxis, is made up of two independent clauses joined by a coordinating conjunction (*and*):

> "I hear and I forget; I see and I remember; I do and I understand." (Confucius)

Freight train

A freight train has three or more independent clauses, usually in the same grammatical pattern, used to shed equal weight on a series of events, ideas, or impressions; to suggest the pure flow of experience; or to simulate the mind's stream of consciousness. As an example, consider the following excerpt from the journal of the painter, Emily Carr, which she wrote while she was out in the wilderness, after five days of teeming rain, alone (except for her dogs and monkey) in her "elephant," a grey and lumbering caravan:

"The rain pours. have put us in and pulled us out until I feel like a worn concertina . . . . But at last, the fire began to burn the sticks, the kettle began to boil the sun began to shine, and I began a new chapter." (*The Journals of Emily Carr*.

Complex sentence

A complex sentence has at least one independent clause, plus one dependent clause. A subordinating conjunction subordinates the dependent clause to the main or independent clause. The clauses are *not* of equal significance. William van Horne, who was in charge of building Canada's first railroad, once said:

main (independent) clause   dependent clause

s/v   s. conj.   s/v

"*The biggest things are* always the easiest to do because *there is* never any competition."

Compound-complex sentence

A compound-complex sentence has at least *two* independent clauses (forming the compound sentence) and at least one dependent clause (forming the complex sentence):

independent clause   s. conj.   dependent clause c. conj.

"Glance into the world just as though time were gone: and

independent clause

everything crooked will become straight to you." (Friedrich Nietzsche)

In order to see the clauses more readily, identify the subject/verb connections. The first clause, an independent clause, is an imperative, so the subject (*you*) is omitted; the second clause is the dependent clause forming the complex (*just as though time were gone*); the third clause is another independent clause forming the compound: *everything crooked will become straight to you.*

Fragment

A fragment is often considered, by teachers, a grammatical mistake; and it is—if used unwittingly. However, good writers will consciously employ fragments. *Fowler's Modern English Usage* lists six uses or purposes for "the verbless sentence" (675):

- transitional—a summary comment on what has gone before or an introduction of what is to come: *Lastly the poetry of metaphor.*
- after thought—in which the use of a full stop suggests a pause for reflection: *Well almost.*
- dramatic climax—*The winter seas endlessly hammering, endlessly probing for a weakness had found one. The cement.*

- comment—especially if playful or strident or intended to surprise. *At the end of the book he goes down into the pit and describes the agony of the work at the coal face. Brilliant. Searing.*
- pictorial—to create or enhance a visual image: *Here silence and beauty were absolute. No aeroplane. Not even trees.*
- aggressive—Fowler describes a school of journalism: *Defying the conventions. Hastening the inevitable social change. Cocking a snook at the hoary traditions and pomposities of our times. Fighting the taboos.* Notice that these are all participial phrases.

In your own writing, if you want to use a fragment for effect, ensure that it does not interfere with your tone or meaning.

(See also **tone**.)

Long sentences

In certain cases, very long sentences can be effective, as long as the reader can clearly follow the writer's train of thought. Recently, Nigel Tomm set the record for the longest sentence in English literature. His book *The Blah Story* (volume four) consists of a single sentence that is 469,375 words (2,273,551 characters) in length ("Longest Sentence"). The following summary is from a 2007 press release:

> Traditionally, the longest sentence in English literature has been found in James Joyce's "Ulysses," which contains 4,391 words. However, this was surpassed in 2001 by Jonathan Coe's book "The Rotter's Club," which contains a sentence 13,955 words long. There is also a Polish novel, "Gates of Paradise," written by Jerzy Andrzejewski, and published in 1960, with [a sentence that contains] about 40,000 words . . . . Finally, there is a Czech novel that consists of one long sentence (128 pages long)—"Dancing Lessons for the Advanced in Age" by Bohumil Hrabal.

Tone

We discussed tone in lesson 18, but here are some additional tips to help you improve your own writing. In your essay writing, avoid using the following types of tone:

- *too tentative*—created by hedging your bets and using qualifiers (*it appears that*) instead of simply stating your point and defending it with evidence;
- *too forceful*—created by overstating your claims instead of presenting evidence;
- *too emotive*—created by using sentimental language, exaggeration, or language that is overly poetic;

- *too informal*—created by using language of the speaking voice rather than the written voice; that is, slang, jargon, contractions, fragments, or too many simple sentences;
- *too authoritative*—created by underestimating the intelligence of your reader; that is, speaking down to the reader, repeating the obvious, explaining the obvious, or, on the other hand, using pretentious diction, attempting to sound more erudite than you are (this invariably sounds false).

In most cases, instructors expect a tone that is measured, formal, usually objective, and modest but confident—a delicate balance, I'll grant you, but a balance that is worth achieving.

Your choice of *point of view* also affects your tone. Choose your point of view carefully. The third-person singular is the obvious choice for a formal essay. However, some subjects will be better suited to the first person. If in doubt, discuss this matter with your instructor.

Quotation Analysis

Legend: Bold for subject, italic for predicate, bold and italic for both part of subject and part of predicate, underline for phrases, bracket for clauses, ALL CAPS for parallel constructions (of words, phrases, or clauses), regular type for fragments and interjections

adj. = adjective, adv. = adverb, art. = article, aux. = auxiliary verb, c. adv. = conjunctive adverb, c. conj. = coordinating conjunction, n. = noun, pro. = pronoun, prep. = preposition, s. = subject, s. conj. = subordinating conjunction, v. = verb; verbals: part. = participle, inf. = infinitive; * = ellipsis

#1 Jane Austen

Simple sentence, indicative mood

pro. aux.   v.   art. adj.   n.   adj. pro. n. prep.   n.   s. conj. adv.
I *have been a selfish being, all my life,* <u>IN PRACTICE</u>, *though not*
prep.   n.
<u>IN PRINCIPLE</u>.

#2 Franz Kafka

Simple sentence, indicative mood

art. n.   aux.   v. s. conj. art.   n. prep. art.   adj.   n.   prep. pro.
A book *should serve* <u>as   the axe   for the frozen sea</u> <u>within us</u>.

#3 Margaret Atwood

Simple sentence, indicative mood

art. n. prep. art. n.   adv.   v. prep. adj.   n.
An eye <u>**for an eye**</u> *only leads* <u>to more blindness</u>.

#4 James Joyce

Compound-complex sentences, indicative + subjunctive moods

pro. aux.   v.   pro. s. conj. pro. aux.   v. c. conj. s. conj. pro. aux. adv.   v. pro. aux.   adv.
I *WILL tell you* (WHAT **I** *WILL do*) *and* (WHAT **I** *WILL not do*). **I** *WILL not*
v. s. conj. prep s. conj. pro.   adv.   v.   s. conj. pro. v.   pro. pro.   n.
serve (that in which **I** *no longer believe*) (whether **it** *call itself* MY HOME,
pro.   n.   c. conj. pro.   n.   c. conj. pro. aux.   v.   inf.   pro.
MY FATHERLAND, *or* MY CHURCH): *and* **I** *WILL try* <u>to express myself</u>

prep. adj.   n.   prep. n. c. conj. n.   adv.   adv. s. conj. pro. v.   c. conj. adv.   adv.   s. conj.
in some mode cf LIFE *or* ART *(AS FREELY AS* **I** *CAN) and (AS WHOLLY AS*

pro. v.   part. prep. pro.   n.   art. adj. n.   pro. v.   pro.   inf.   n.
I *CAN,* using for my defense *the only arms (*I allow myself to use, SILENCE,*

n.   c. conj.   n.
EXILE, and CUNNING).

* = that (subordinating conjunction)

#5 Dylan Thomas

Simple sentence, indicative mood
Accumulation of finite verbs tied to the subject: great gods

part.   c. conj.   part.   adj.   adj.   adj.   n. prep. art.
LOLLING AND LARRICKING that unsoiled, boiling beauty of a

adj.   n.   adj.   n.   prep. pro.   n.   prep. pro.   n.   v.
common day, great gods with their braces over their vests *sang,*

v. n.   v.   n. prep. n.   v.   c. conj. v.   v.   art. n.
spat pips, puffed smoke at wasps, *GULPED AND OGLED, forgot the rent,*

v.   v. prep. art.   n.   v.   adj. v.   adj.
embraced, posed for the dicky-bird, *were coarse, had rainbow-coloured*

n.   v.   v.   v.   art.   n.   v. prep.   n.
armpits, WINKED, BELCHED, blamed the radishes, looked at Ilfracombe,

v.   n. prep. n. c. conj. n.   v.   n.   v.   v.
played hymns on PAPER AND COMB, *peeled bananas, scratched, found*

n. prep. pro. n.   v. adv. adj. n. c. conj. v.   pro.   v.
seaweed in their panamas, *blew up paper bags and banged them, wished*

prep. noun.
for nothing.

#6 Pearl Buck

Simple sentences: indicative, imperative, indicative

art.   n.   v. adv.   adj.   v. pro. c. adv. n. v. adj. prep. pro.
The truth *is always exciting. Speak* **it**, *then.* **Life** *is dull* without it.

#7 Simone de Beauvoir

Complex sentence, subjunctive mood

pro. v. s. conj. adj.   adj.   n.   aux. v. adj.   adj.
I *wish (that* **EVERY HUMAN LIFE** *might be PURE TRANSPARENT*

n.
FREEDOM).

#8 Gabriel Garcia Marquez

Simple sentence, indicative mood

art.   n.   prep. pro.   n.   prep.   n.   adv. pro. adj.
The interpretation of our reality through patterns not our own,
    v.   adv.   inf. v. pro. adv.   adv.   adj.   adv.   adv.   adj.   adv.
serves only to make us EVER MORE UNKNOWN, EVER LESS FREE, EVER
adv.   adj.
MORE SOLITARY.

#9 André Gide

Simple sentence, indicative mood

      n.   aux. adv.   v.   adj.   n.   prep.   part.   inf. v.   n.
One _does not discover new lands_ without consenting _to lose sight_
prep. art.   n. prep. art. adv. adj.   n.
of the shore for a very long time.

#10 Heraclitus

Compound sentence, indicative mood

        n.   v.   n.   v.
(EVERYTHING _FLOWS_); (**NOTHING** _REMAINS_).

#11 Oscar Wilde

Compound sentence, indicative mood

   pro. adj.   n.   adv.   v. pro. prep. n. pro. v.   adj.   n. (possessive)
My own business _always bores me to death;_ I _prefer other people's._

Note: There is an ellipsis at the end of the sentence (business).

#12 Virginia Woolf

Compound sentence, interrogative mood

   v. pro. adj.   v. pro. adj.   v. pro. adj. conj. adj.
_(IS_ **IT** _GOOD), (IS_ **IT** _BAD), (IS_ **IT** _RIGHT or WRONG)?_

Consider the last clause balanced rather than parallel (exact grammatical pattern). 'Right' and 'wrong' are parallel words.

#13 Graham Greene

Complex sentence, indicative mood

    s. conj. pro. v. adv. adj.   pro. v.   adj.
(When **WE** _are not sure),_ (**WE** _are alive)._

Consider these two clauses balanced rather than parallel.

#14 Hannah Arendt

Complex sentence, indicative mood

art. adj.   n.   v.   s. conj. adj.   n.   aux. v.   prep.   n.   s. conj.   adv.   v.   adv.

The sad truth is (that **most evil** is done by people) (**who** never make up

pro.   n.   inf. v.   adv.   adj.   c. conj.   adj.

their minds to be either GOOD OR EVIL).

#15 Martin Luther King Jr.

Complex sentence, indicative mood

art.   adj.   n.   prep.   n.   aux.   v.   prep.   pro.   s. conj.   v.   adj.

The hottest place in Hell is reserved for those (**who** remain neutral

prep.   n.   prep.   adj.   adj.   n.

in times of great moral conflict).

#16 Johann Wolfgang von Goethe

Complex sentence, indicative mood

absolute phrase   s. conj.   aux.   v.   prep.   n.   v.   n.   prep.   n.

FIRST AND LAST, (**what is demanded of genius**) is love of truth).

#17 David Suzuki

Compound, complex; indicative mood

pro. v.   prep. art.   adj.   n.   part.   prep.   art. adj.   n.   conj.

We're   in   a   giant car heading towards a brick wall, and

pro.   v.   part.   prep.   s. conj.   pro. v.   part.   inf.

everyone's arguing over where **they**'re going to sit.

#18 Barbara Gowdy

Simple, complex, fragment; indicative mood

pro.   n.   v.   adj.   prep. adj.   n.   pro. aux.   v.   prep.

My memory is photographic, in living colour. (**I**'m flooded with

n.   adv.   n.   prep.   n.   pro. aux.   v.   art.   adj.   n.   prep.

memories, mostly images from dreams) (**I**'ve had). A leather jacket with

adj.   n.   part.   n.   adj.   c. conj.   part.   n.   part.

four tulips, eating blueberries half blind and having blueberries scattered

prep. art.   n.   part.   n.   s. conj.   v.   adv.   inf.   n.   n.   adj.

on the ground, growing limbs (that turn out to be tree limbs, useless).

#19 Angela Carter

Complex sentence, indicative mood

n.   v.   pro. adj.   n. prep. pro. n.   prep. art.   n. prep. n. c. conj.

(Aeneas carried his aged father on his back from the ruins of Troy) and

c. conj. v. pro. adj.   s. conj.   pro.   v. pro. c. conj. adv.   adv.   adv. s. conj.

(so do **we** all), (whether **we** like it or not), (perhaps even if

pro. aux.   adv.   v.   pro.

we have never known them).

#22 George Elliott Clarke

Complex sentence, indicative mood

adj.   n.   pro. v.   pro.   adj.   n.   pro.   n. prep.   n.

Black Madonna! **I** love YOUR AFRICAN ESSENCE, YOUR FAITH IN CHILDREN,

pro.   adj.   n.   prep.   n.   pro.   adj.   n.

YOUR INSATIABLE DESIRE FOR FREEDOM, YOUR SWIFT INTELLIGENCE,

pro.   adj.   n.   pro.   adj.   n.   pro.   n.

YOUR SHARP PASSION, YOUR SECRET STRENGTHS, YOUR LANGUAGE

s. conj.   v.   adj.   n.   pro.   n.   s. conj. v.   n.   pro.   n.

(THAT TELLS NO LIES), YOUR FASHION (THAT IS COLOUR), YOUR MUSIC

s. conj.   v. (compound) n.   pro.   n. prep.   adj.   n.   pro.

(THAT IS GOSPEL-LULLABY), YOUR LIPS LIKE CRIMSON BERRIES, YOUR

n.   prep.   adj.   adj.   n.   pro.   n. prep.   n.   pro.   n.

SKIN LIKE SOFT, MOIST NIGHT, YOUR EYES LIKE DUSK, YOUR HAIR

prep.   adj.   n.   pro.   n.   prep. adj.   n.   pro.   n.

LIKE DARK COTTON, YOUR SCENT LIKE RICH BUTTER, YOUR TASTE

prep.   n.   c. conj.   n. c. conj. adj.   n.

LIKE RAISINS AND DATES AND SWEET WINE.

Note that there are three different balanced constructions: 1) pronoun (possessive adjective your), adjective, noun; 2) pronoun, noun, prepositional phrase; and 3) pronoun, noun, that clause. However, not all the phrases or clauses are exact in the number of adjectives.

#23 Simone Weil

Complex sentence, indicative mood

s. conj. pro.   n.   prep.   n.   v.   prep.   n.   inf.   verbal   adj.

(Even if **our efforts of attention** seem for years to be producing no

n.   adj. n. art. n. s. conj. v. prep. adj.   n.   prep. pro. aux.

result), (one day **a light [that is in exact proportion to them]** will

v.   art.   n.

flood the soul.)

Works Cited

Abrams, M.H. *A Glossary of Literary Terms*. 7th ed. Boston: Heinle & Heinle Publishers, 1998. Print.

Arnold, G.L. Untitled. *The Twentieth Century* 151 (1952). Print.

Blaise, Clarke. "To Begin to Begin." *The Narrative Voice: Short Stories and Reflections by Canadian Authors*. Ed. John Metcalf. Toronto: McGraw, 1972. 22–26. Print.

Clarke, George Elliott. *Blue*. Vancouver: Raincoast Books, 2001. Print.

———. "The Critique of African-Canadian Literature." *Journal of Canadian Studies* (April 2004): 5–8. Print.

Copland, Aaron. *What to Listen for in Music*. New York: Penguin Putnam Inc., 1999. Print.

Dalhousie University. "Introduction to Peter Sanger's Honorary Degree." Dalhousie University. 2012. Convocation. Web.

de Certeau, Michel. *Culture in the Plural*. Trans. Tom Conley. Minneapolis: University of Minnesota Press, 1997. Print.

Dillard, Annie. *For the Time Being*. Toronto: Penguin Books, 2000. Print.

Donaghy, Henry J. *Graham Greene: An Introduction to His Writings*. Amsterdam: Rodopi, 1983. Print.

Eagleton, Terry. *Literary Theory*. Minneapolis: University of Minnesota Press, 1983. Print.

Enkvist, Nils Erik, John Spencer, Michael J. Gregory. *Linguistics and Style*. London: Oxford University Press, 1971. Print.

Fowler, Henry Watson. *Modern English Usage*. 2nd ed. Ed. Ernest Gowers. Oxford: Oxford University Press, 1968. Print.

Freud, Sigmund. "The Dissection of the Psychical Personality." *New Introductory Lectures on Psycho-Analysis*. Ed. James Strachey. New York: W.W. Norton & Company Ltd., 1990. 71–100. Print.

Graham, Daniel W. "Heraclitus." *The Stanford Encyclopedia of Philosophy*. Ed. Edward N. Zalta, Fall 2008. Web. 20 Nov. 2009.

Hemingway, Ernest. Interview by George Plimpton. "The Art of Fiction No. 21," *The Paris Review* Interview, 1958. Web.

Iwama, Marilyn, Murdena Marshall, Albert Marshall, Ivar Mendez, and Cheryl Bartlett. *I Got It from an Elder: Conversations in Healing Language*. Kentville, NS: Gaspereau Press, 2008. Print.

Glenn, Joshua. "Simone Weil, 1909–1943." *Hermenaut* 20 Nov. 2009. Web.

Kane, Thomas, and Heather Pyrcz. *The Canadian Oxford Guide to Writing: A Rhetoric and Handbook*. 2nd ed. Don Mills: Oxford University Press Canada, 2008. Print.

Kaveney, Roz. "Angela Carter Remembered." *TimeOut London*, 30 May 2006. Web. 20 Nov. 2009.

Kunitz, Stanley, and Howard Haycroft, eds. *British Authors of the Nineteenth Century*. New York: H.W. Wilson, 1936. Print.

Levin, Harry. "James Joyce." *The Atlantic Monthly*, December 1946. Web. 20 Nov. 2009.

"Longest Sentence in English Literature/Language." *PRLog*. Web. 22 Nov. 2007.

Lucas, F.L. *Style*. London: Cassell, 1955. Print.

McGuirk, Bernard, and Richard Cardwell, eds. *Gabriel Garcia Marquez: New Readings*. Cambridge: Cambridge University Press, 1987. Print.

Orwell, George. "Politics and the English Language." *Horizon* 13.76 (1946): 252–65. Print.

Peach, Linden. "Angela Carter." *The Literary Encyclopedia*, 15 March 2001. Web. 20 Nov. 2009.

Pound, Ezra. *ABC of Reading*. New York: New Directions Publishing, 1960. Print.

———. "Past History." *The Letters of Ezra Pound to James Joyce*. Ed. Forrest Read. New York: New Directions Publishing, 1965. 245–59. Print.

Schmidt, Michael. *Lives of the Poets*. New York: Knopf, 1999. Print.

Scholes, Robert, Nancy R. Comley, and Gregory L. Ulmer. *Text Book: An Introduction to Literary Language*. 2nd ed. New York: St. Martin's Press, 1995. 46–57. Print.

Sontag, Susan. "Simone Weil." *The New York Review of Books* 1.1 (1 Feb. 1963). Web. 20 Nov. 2009.

Weil, Simone. *Gravity and Grace*. London: Routledge and Kegan Paul, 1952. Print.

Wells, Zachariah. "Aiken Drum." Rev. of *Aiken Drum* by Peter Sanger. *Quill and Quire*. May 2006: 52. Print/Web.

Yar, Majid. "Hannah Arendt (1906–1975)." *The Internet Encyclopedia of Philosophy*. Eds. James Fieser and Bradley Dowden, 2006. Web. 20 Nov. 2009.

Index